JODIE'S STORY

'Tell them that there is no pit so deep that he is not deeper still.'

Betsie ten Boom
From *The Hiding Place*
by Corrie ten Boom

JODIE'S STORY

Jeanette Grant-Thomson

REGENT COLLEGE PUBLISHING
VANCOUVER

JODIE'S STORY
Copyright © 1991 Jeanette Grant-Thomson

First published by 1991 by
ANZEA Publishers
3-5 Richmond Road
Homebush West NSW
2140 Australia

This edition published 2003 by
Regent College Publishing
5800 University Boulevard
Vancouver, BC V6T 2E4 Canada
www.regentpublishing.com

All rights reserved. No part of this book may be reproduced in any form without permission in writing from the publisher, except by a reviewer who may quote brief passages in a review to be printed in a magazine or newspaper.

Views expressed in works published by Regent College Publishing are those of the author and do not necessarily represent the views or opinions of Regent College. For more information about Regent College visit our website at: www.regent-college.edu

ISBN 1-57383-249-9

Foreword

Many of us are familiar with the dramatic American Teen Challenge stories, David Wilkerson's *The Cross and the Switchblade* and Nicky Cruz's *Run, Baby Run*. The Australian Teen Challenge story has never been told, but part of its telling, in the deeply human *Jodie's Story*, forms an interesting contrast to the American counterparts.

Jodie is not one of the outstanding successes of the Brisbane Teen Challenge programme. She is one of the many ordinary troubled and drug-dependent young people who came to us for help and stayed long enough to find a new life in Christ. The author has therefore done us a great service. She has moved from the spectacular to the ordinary, but has made the ordinary spectacular. For in the Jodie Cadman story we meet a young woman in her struggle to overcome grief and hardship. We feel her pain, understand her struggles and are dismayed by the folly of her choices and lifestyle. We can join with her in her groping for answers and her struggle to come to faith and wholeness.

In this sense, Jodie's story is everyone's story. And particularly so in that she is not a heroine in the Christian Church. She has become a mother and not a full-time evangelist. Yet her life sparkles with the miraculous. Her journey to faith, her healing and her vibrant love for God all speak of the wonderful grace of God. Jeanette Grant-Thomson has not only given us a story full of courage and hope but a book that should be put into the hands of every young person who struggles with life and looks to drugs as a way out.

Charles Ringma

The Reverend Charles Ringma was the founder of Teen Challenge in Australia and the Executive-Director of Teen Challenge Queensland for its first thirteen years.

Contents

Foreword	v
Preface	ix
Acknowledgments	xi
One	1
Two	7
Three	25
Four	37
Five	45
Six	55
Seven	67
Eight	71
Nine	81
Ten	95
Eleven	111
Twelve	127
Thirteen	133
Fourteen	139
Fifteen	155
Epilogue	163

Preface

When I first met Jodie, I was surprised. I had heard parts of her story and formed a mental picture of someone thin and sickly, loudly-spoken and a bit rough or 'cheap' looking. Instead, I answered the door to a warm, friendly girl with a lively personality. A sincere Christian. She quickly endeared herself to my whole family. There was little, if any, visible scar from her former lifestyle.

I interviewed her initially for over three hours. As she told me her story, I fought tears several times.

This book is, essentially, the true story of the girl who was known to the world of crime and prostitution as *Jodie Cadman*. Some of the minor characters and events are fictitious and I have changed the names of some of the characters to protect Jodie and her family and friends. All the major events and many of the minor ones, nearly all the emotions expressed by Jodie, and the actual story are completely true—the good, the supernatural, and the horrific. Jodie Cadman was Jodie's actual *street name* and perhaps some of you who read this book knew her. Several of the 1982–3 Teen Challenge staff—Charles Ringma (then Executive Director of Teen Challenge, Brisbane) and his wife Rita, Neil and Sue Paulsen, Margie Shanahan and Jill Hall—have given me permission to use their real names and to locate that part of the story in the Teen Challenge environment as it was at that time.

I have not used the authentic street language that many of the characters actually would have used, as I felt this type of swearing would be a deterrent to some readers. I have used some words that give a suggestion of language which would have been much more colourful.

I thank God for his mercy in intervening as Jodie sank in the quicksand of sin and desperation, and in transforming her into a radiant Christian. I pray for all the 'Jodies' (and the 'Jonothans' and 'Roxys') still out there, that they too may come to know him, who brought peace and happiness to Jodie Cadman.

Acknowledgments

I want to thank first of course, Jodie, for permission to use her life story so far and her real 'street name'.

My thanks also to Charles and Rita Ringma, Neil and Sue Paulsen, Margie Shanahan, Jill and Albert Hall and all the Teen Challenge staff for permission to use their names, for patiently recounting various memories of Jodie, and for allowing me to locate the story where it actually took place—in the Teen Challenge setting.

My sincere thanks to my sister, Arlene, who patiently typed this manuscript and acted as my sounding board.

Finally, my thanks go again to Charles Ringma for his constructive criticism and help.

Chapter One

Jonothan was dead. I flung myself over the white hospital bed, and clutched his body frantically. He could not be dead. He looked so perfect, as he always had. Not a drop of blood on him, his quiet face peaceful in its final rest. Not for my dignified brother, Jonothan, the ugly death of a mangled body and oozing blood. Not even in a bike accident.

Someone was screaming hysterically. The anguished 'No, no, no!' sounded strangely distant. I realised I was the one screaming. But nothing seemed real. Nothing except Jonothan, lying there. Jonothan, dead. I was vaguely aware of white-clad forms moving around me, and some men—hospital staff, I suppose—pulled me away from Jonothan.

Help me, somebody. They're taking me away from him. My body is going with them but inside I'm not there. I'm dead, like Jonothan. He was the only person left I loved. He cared. Cared enough to try to stop my drunken rages and my sleeping with the boys in the bike gang. Jonothan is my only link with reality; my only reason to live. And they're dragging me away from him. Everything seems confused, far away. Help me, somebody.

I groped my way through the next few days in shock. My mind still refused to accept what had happened.

Ironically, it had been my mother who had first brought me the news. My mother, that embittered little woman who made me feel so angry. She had appeared in the doorway of the flat where I lived with Ray. She stood there, a white-faced figure, and simply said, 'It's Jonothan,' and I knew. I screamed hysterically.

How can he be dead? Only a few hours ago I was talking to him. He rode past me on his bike and I waved proudly. I wasn't waving goodbye, so he can't be dead.

But Jonothan was dead. On a clear, sunny, late winter's day he had ridden his bike, enjoying the exhilaration of the crisp New Zealand air. Blinded by the setting sun, he had crashed into a car and been thrown off his bike.

'Broken neck,' they said.

I walked out of my flat in a daze and never went back. Just like that. I walked out of my relationship with Ray. I walked out of my job; out of everything. Out of reality.

The only reality left for me was my memories of Jonothan. So I went back and lived at my mother's place and slept in his room. Frantically I unearthed every photograph of him, all his possessions. I arrayed them all around the room. It became a shrine to Jonothan. I started wearing some of his clothes, savouring that special smell that was him. Clutching at his very identity.

I floated numbly through the funeral, the encounters with relatives, and the meetings with his bikie friends in a blur. Whenever reality threatened to intrude on my consciousness, I blotted it out quickly in the now-familiar ways—drugs and alcohol. Bikers from hundreds of miles away came home for the funeral. The whole district, everyone who knew him, came. Jonothan was someone who had quietly won people's respect.

We were a rough crowd. At a party soon after the funeral, when I was stumbling around in a haze of dope, pills and alcohol, one of Jonothan's old friends tried to rape me. I wanted to be sick—my own brother's friend, and my brother just dead. It was hideous, but so was everything now.

For a few weeks I lived in my brother's room, wearing his clothes, living him, hanging onto him. I went out only to get drunk. I would wake in the morning with a gnawing emptiness inside me, and quickly grab some pills or a drink.

One morning I awoke sobbing. I felt empty. I couldn't bear it. There was a hollowness even to my shrine. A hollowness I could no longer escape.

There was a knock at the bedroom door. It was Mum.

'Jodie, for heaven's sake, snap out of it,' she spat at me. 'You won't bring him back by trying to look like him. He's gone, girl, gone. Stop torturing yourself and me.'

'Oh shut up, Mum,' I retorted.

'Well you're not staying here like this in my home. You can get out and find yourself a job.' She threw a paper onto the bed. It was open at the 'Positions Vacant' section.

I gazed at it uncaringly. One advertisement caught my eye. It was a job in a drug warehouse. I threw on a blouse with my jeans, combed my hair, and went for the interview. I must have fooled the guy because I got the job.

It was a drug-user's paradise. I did only the minimum of routine work, and helped myself to drugs packaged ready to supply chemists. Every evening I'd go home with my bag and blouse almost bulging with drugs. I had found a real source of income—I became a dealer. Drugs of all types were freely available and I took them myself as well as dealing them. Everything, even opium. Who cared? Anything to make reality retreat to a bearable distance. I just didn't care. I wanted to annihilate myself.

One night at a party I met Pete, a man who was leaving for Sydney the next day. I went to the airport to see him off, stoned out of my brain on opium. People stared at me, barefooted and bedraggled. I gazed back numbly.

God, what am I doing here? There are people rushing, rushing everywhere. They're all going somewhere. I'm not going anywhere. I don't belong anywhere. There's nothing, no-one left I care about. God, if you exist, why did you put me in this hell-life? What have I done to deserve it?

Pete sensed my desolation. And perhaps my potential. 'Why don't you come?' he asked.

'Why not?' I thought. 'I've got nothing to lose.' He gave me the money and I bought a ticket. Was it significant that it was the last seat left?

Soon I was sitting, still in a haze, watching the houses of Auckland dwindle to little boxes below me. I settled back in my seat and almost enjoyed it. It was only the second time in my twenty years that I'd left New Zealand. Perhaps things would get better now.

As my mind wandered idly over my life, and as the opium began to wear off a bit, I realised I was sitting with my fists clenched, as one of my frequent waves of rage welled up inside me. The rage that had driven me fiercely through most of my life. I had almost forgotten why I was angry. Almost, but not quite.

Chapter Two

I had never quite forgotten my mother's words overheard when I was six. The day began like any other day in my six-year-old world. It was the summer holidays at the end of my first year's school. I woke to a brisk fresh breeze and bright blue skies, and was soon out playing with Susan and Margie Johnson from next door. Our small back lawn, with its low fences, seemed quite big to us, and we would invent all sorts of wonderful games and adventures, usually centring around the large white-flowering tree at the foot of the garden.

Like most of the families in our street, we had little money for expensive toys or games. It was one of the poorer areas of a small town in the

North Island of New Zealand. But none of that bothered us. We were content in our play-world.

This particular day was unusually hot and I slipped inside for a drink. I was at the fridge when I realised my mother was talking to Mrs Johnson in the adjacent loungeroom. Being a curious child, I listened. At first it was hard to hear what they were saying, but suddenly I heard my name. I crept over and put my ear to the wall. My mother was talking. 'I can't bear to touch Jodie. I wish I'd never had a girl. She just revolts me, somehow.'

I couldn't move. In a few seconds, my whole world had changed. I huddled, white-faced and shaking, against the wall, trying not to cry. My throat and jaw ached with the effort of suppressing sobs.

There was more, but I hardly heard it. Something about a baby boy she had had adopted as a teenager, and another baby boy whom she described as 'stillborn'. I wondered what this meant, and guessed it might mean the baby had died, as my only brothers were younger than I was, and she was talking about much earlier days.

Mummy, why don't you love me? Is it because I'm a girl? Aren't girls as nice as boys? Is that why you never hug me? I don't understand. I'm frightened.

My supposedly secure world had collapsed

around me. Happy times at the dinner table, holding my mother's (reluctant?) hand on the way to the shop, playing mummies and daddies with my dolls, and the many innocently expectant thoughts of childhood, all crumbled in a heap at my feet like a pack of cards as if they'd been only cards, pictures, illusions, anyway. I wanted to run away, but where could I go?

There was a shuffle and a rattle of cups from the loungeroom. Terror of being discovered there with my tear-streaked face overwhelmed me, and I tiptoed quickly on shaking legs to the back door and ran outside. Susie and her sister must have grown tired of waiting for me and gone home, much to my relief. I ran and climbed the old tree and hid up there, crying until there were no more tears. Eventually, as the late twilight grew darker and I began to shiver, I climbed down and went inside for tea.

Nobody noticed how quiet I was at the table because Dad had been drinking again. He rambled on, without waiting for answers, while Mum stared at him resentfully. Jonothan, who was five, was my favourite brother. He kicked me under the table when Dad started on a story we'd all heard several times before. I pretended not to notice and busied myself with my vegetables. Roger, the youngest, was happily eating in his highchair, oblivious to all the tensions.

The hurt grew inside me like an ulcer and I began to hate both my parents. How dare my mother not love me? She was my mother. And

Dad was just as bad. He came home drunk more and more often as I grew up, and he seemed almost unaware of us kids.

Mum loved Jonothan and Roger. I'd often see her cuddling them fondly. I craved the same affection and sometimes ran up to her wanting a hug, but she always pushed me away. It was confusing. I would go to my room and cry for hours after my mother's rebuffs, still not really understanding it all. Seeing her shower affection on my brothers, I started to try to be like them, hoping to win my mother's acceptance and love. I began to act and dress like a real tomboy, and one day dressed in one of Jonothan's shorts and T-shirt outfits. I grinned tentatively at my boyish reflection in the mirror. With my tanned face and short hair, I could easily pass for a boy. I slipped out to the breakfast table. Surely, surely she would like me now?

'Jodie! What the hell are you doing in your brother's clothes? You go and get changed straight away. Cheeky little brat.' My mother's words fell like an explosion on my ears. With drooping shoulders, I walked slowly from the room and changed.

Mum and Dad fought most of the time, too. Dad continued to come home drunk, often well after tea at night. But most of the parents in our district fought, so I didn't worry much about it. I had no idea how serious their problems were.

After years of craving affection and being abruptly denied it, my hatred and anger grew beyond my control. One Saturday I was ironing and Mum and Dad were talking on the comfortable old chairs nearby. Suddenly violent rage welled up inside me for no apparent reason, and I hurled the hot iron at Dad. I missed, but he was furious. He shouted at me, so I grabbed a chair and threw it at him, then another one at Mum, hardly knowing what I was doing. A blinding white-hot fury filled my being.

My father grabbed me and slapped me. I slapped him back. So he flung me into the chair where he'd been sitting. The rage subsided and left me white-faced and trembling, but still filled with a sullen anger that I barely understood.

That was the first of many such outbursts. I was thirteen now. My bewildered parents took me to a doctor and soon each day began with a valium tablet in an abortive attempt to control my turbulent nature.

My confusion and frustration grew. My father was drinking more heavily by the time I was fourteen. Unknown to us, he had resorted to dishonesty in his business, and was probably trying to blot out his guilt.

One night in particular stands out in my memory. We'd gone to bed about ten o'clock, after watching one of our favourite television shows. In between my outbursts of anger, Jonothan, Roger and I enjoyed one another's company. Mum had gone to bed earlier, exhausted, and left us laughing at an English comedy.

The boys must have fallen asleep soon after we went to our rooms, because their giggling and whispering quickly died away. The house was silent. It was a windy night and the peach tree outside my window rattled against the glass panes eerily. I lay there sleepless. Suddenly a car door slammed, followed by the crash of the front door being kicked open. It must be Dad. Sounded like he was well and truly drunk tonight. I pulled the bedcovers closely around my chin and tried to ignore the noises and the ghastly images they conjured.

There was another crash and a loud thud. I leapt out of bed, frightened, and peered over the bannisters. There in the hallway lay Dad, quite still. I ran down the steps wondering if he was dead.

The stench of urine almost sickened me as I crept up to him. He wasn't dead, just unconscious. I looked at him with a mixture of pity and revulsion. But he was my father, so I summoned all my strength and hauled him over onto the sofa.

It took several washings with warm soapy water to get the smell off my hands. Finally, I returned to bed, but sleep would not come. I lay in a waking nightmare.

Dad continued to come home drunk at all hours. Sometimes Jonothan was awake to help me with him, but I hated my beloved brother to see Dad like this. Jonothan always seemed clean and pure. He stood for everything good in life and was somehow not a part of this ugly situation. I didn't want him to be defiled. Mum never emerged from her room. I think she would have left him lying there on the floor. I realise now she had had as much as she could take.

Life was becoming unbearable. I wished I could go away—anywhere—just to be free from the hideous mess at home. Gradually a plan began to form. I would run away. I'd set off one morning in my school uniform with my lunch, all my saved pocket money, and a change of clothes in my bag. My only hesitation was about leaving Jonothan. Would he be all right?

The planned day arrived. I was dressed early and ate a huge breakfast to keep me going as long as possible.

'Well, it's not like you to be ready early,' said Mum sarcastically.

'What's on today, Jode?' asked Jonothan.

'Oh, we've got hockey practice before school,' I lied. 'I'm getting the early bus.'

'I'll hurry and come with you.' Jonothan's voice was eager.

For a few seconds I panicked, but a quick look at my watch reassured me. 'Too late, Jono,' I smiled, hating myself for betraying his trust. 'Another day, maybe.'

I walked down the front path, trying to look as if it was like any other school day. Soon I was around the corner and out of sight.

Freedom! Man, this is unreal! I can go anywhere I like. Do anything. Mum and Dad will be glad to see the back of me. No more broken windows and flying furniture! Jonothan, who's going to look after you? I guess you'll be all right. At least Mum cares about you. I'll miss you, Jono. No-one else.

Soon Kathy was in sight. She'd promised to take the day off school to take me to her bikie friends. I'd always been slightly in awe of Kathy. She was a little older and had it together more than I did. She'd already left home, was part of a bike gang, and was leaving school at the end of this year. School . . . I hated it. I wasn't sure if I'd bother to return or not.

'Hi Jodie! Come on, quick. We can't hang around with you in that uniform.'

Trying to look completely cool and grown up, I swallowed the rising tide of apprehension inside me and walked jauntily beside Kathy. Before long we reached an old house which was divided into flats. The yard was overgrown and the house had peeling paint and a few broken windows patched with masking tape and newspaper. I pushed away the memory of my cosy home and walked quickly up the steps.

The house stank of stale beer, smoke and a few unfamiliar smells. Four guys sat in the loungeroom, smoking. They were older than I'd expected—they all looked at least twenty.

Kathy introduced me. One of them, Keith,

seemed very nice and friendly. He smiled and winked at me.

'Better get changed, Jodie.' Kathy led me to a filthy bathroom and I changed into the jeans and T-shirt I'd stuffed into my school bag.

'Here.' The tallest boy, who seemed like the leader, handed me a glass of beer. 'You can stay here for a few days at least. We'll see, then.'

I said as little as possible that day, trying to conceal my ignorance. Some of the terms sounded familiar. Kathy had used them at school, describing her adventures. And I already knew that 'grass' and 'pot' were marijuana.

That evening, more people arrived. It seemed that it was a party, although nothing had been said about it. Most of the girls wore jeans and T-shirts, but a few arrived looking glamorous or quaint. One girl wore a black lace dress with nothing at all underneath it. Through my unaccustomed haze of alcohol, it all seemed unreal, like watching a movie.

Keith was often at my side and grew more friendly with each drink and each joint of marijuana. About ten o'clock he led me into one of the bedrooms and I realised sex was part of the deal with a bike gang. That was okay; I wanted to be cool and independent of my family, and Keith was nice.

The next day I went for a 'run' on the back of Keith's bike. It was great. The cool air rushing onto my face was exhilarating. I couldn't wait till the next ride.

After a few days, Dane, the leader, seemed edgy.

'What's up, mate?' Keith asked.

'Cops were hanging around outside this morning. You'd better get rid of the girl. She's too green.'

'Got anywhere else you can go, Jodie?' asked Keith.

'Only home. But it's okay. I'll go. I don't want to get you into trouble.'

Keith hesitated. 'Can I pick you up from your place sometimes? You can still be my girl.'

'Yeah, okay.' I was glad.

I crept up the back steps at home, hoping to slip in unnoticed. It was midday, and I had no intention of going to school. Luckily, Mum was out working. It was one of her house-cleaning days, which supplied the money for the 'extras' like new clothes and books. I slumped onto my bed and waited uneasily, thinking of various stories I could use on my parents.

Hearing the clatter of dishes on the table, I decided to join the boys for afternoon tea. I walked nonchalantly into the kitchen as if nothing were unusual. One look at Mum's face told me it would be harder than I'd expected.

'Jodie! Where've you been?' Jonathan shouted.

I couldn't wait to tell Jono about my adventure and most of all, bikes, but now was not the time. 'Staying with friends,' I replied in an elaborately casual tone.

'Friends!' My mother's voice cut the tense

atmosphere like a knife blow. 'What sort of friends would put you up without telling your family where you were? I've rung every hospital in the area. And the police. You wait till your father gets home.'

Fortunately for me, things didn't turn out quite as Mum expected. Dad was out drinking again. Finally she sent me to my room.

Mum was very silent and pale for several days. On a freezing cold Thursday night she pulled me aside. 'I'm going to stay with your Aunt Rosie for a few days. Don't know how you'll manage the meals with school and everything, but you'll just have to do your best. If I don't take a break now, it'll be me who's breaking.'

Aunt Rosemary lived in beautiful Queenstown, so Mum flew there the next day. Dad dropped her at the airport and arranged to pick her up on Tuesday evening.

The weekend was like a horror movie. Dad invited all his friends over, and they drank all weekend. Every room was invaded by raucous drunks. In every corner, people were either cuddling, arguing, collapsing in a stupor, or being sick. The boys and I didn't know what to make of it all.

Man, this place is meant to be my home. Some home! I must be going crazy. Or maybe they're all crazy. I'm going to split from this place again as soon as Mum's back.

Monday morning brought the inevitable dreaded return to school. I'd managed to avoid it on Friday by genuinely being sick.

Monday mornings always gave the week a bad flavour by starting with Mrs Marsden's English lesson. She and I clashed in a quiet, cold way. Most of the kids liked her fairly well as she was a pleasant, even-tempered woman and the epitome of respectability. Needless to say, everything about me violated her moral and social standards. That didn't worry me, but I resented her violently because she never understood that I was unhappy and crying out for acceptance. I could have forgiven her hyper-respectability, but she never gave me the chance. Today she had a valid reason for picking on me.

As soon as we were seated, she stared at me icily. 'Jodie, leave the room. Girls who are absent without reason for nearly a week cannot expect to turn up as if nothing has happened. You can go straight to Mr Jones with this note.'

Mr Jones was the headmaster. He sighed and looked at me sadly. 'Well, Jodie, we've tried to be patient with you,' he said in a tired voice. 'This is the last straw, though. Your mother told us she had no idea where you were last week. Girls who behave like that give the school a poor reputation. There have been reports of your smoking marijuana. And you've stretched your teachers to the limit with your insolence. I'm afraid I have no alternative; I must ask you to leave.'

He seemed to be waiting for an answer, but I felt nothing and just stared at him.

'Hopefully this will shock you into turning over a new leaf,' he began again. 'If you're lucky, one of the other schools may take you. I sincerely hope you'll behave better for them than you have for us.'

He dismissed me. I packed my school books and went home. Although I had felt very little during the talk with the headmaster, I now felt strangely depressed.

Pull yourself out of it, Jodie. What the hell? You hated school anyway. You can always get a job. And there's Keith and the bike gang.

I whispered my news to Jonothan when he arrived home. He was genuinely shocked.

The next day was Tuesday. I grabbed Dad before he left for work. He seemed strangely preoccupied.

'What is it? No, of course I haven't forgotten we're getting your mother from the airport. See you later.'

He took longer than usual leaving the house. Finally the door slammed. A strange sense of foreboding made me go to my parents' room. All his belongings were gone. No note, nothing.

That night, he didn't come home. The boys and I asked Mrs Johnson if she'd drive us to the airport. We told her briefly what had happened.

Mum chattered brightly all the way home

from the airport. None of us had the heart to say anything yet. She was happier than we'd seen her for months. We drove in and took her luggage.

A long white envelope had been pushed under the front door. Mum picked it up and opened it quickly. Her face froze with horror.

'What is it, Mum?' Roger's voice was frightened.

'Separation papers. Your father wants a divorce. He's left for good.' Her voice was shaking.

Things grew worse every day after that. Mum was just a heap of bitterness. She took most of her anger out on me. The boys could rarely do wrong in her eyes.

One day she flared up over a trivial incident. Something inside me flared right back and there I was again, in its grip. I grabbed the scissors and threw them at her. Then I began throwing everything in sight. The sound of smashing glass—one of the dining room windows—only aggravated my rage. As suddenly as it had begun, once again, it subsided, leaving me frightened and shaking, drained of all energy. But I'd had enough. I headed off for Keith's place.

'You've got to put me up,' I whispered urgently. 'I'll murder her if I stay there.' They hesitantly agreed.

Keith and I were still sleeping together. Although he was still nice and friendly, a strange hardness and aloofness was developing in him. It scared me. I felt shut out. One night I discovered the cause. As I entered our room, he was shooting up heroin. He was shaking and small beads of perspiration had formed on his forehead. But the drug worked quickly and he was soon the Keith I knew.

You fool, Keith. Heroin's a mug's game. You'll end up dead. Everyone does with that stuff. Grass is okay, but not that rubbish.

A sharp rap at the door startled me. Everyone else was out. Keith grabbed his syringe and headed for the bathroom, calling, 'You get it,' over his shoulder.

It was the police. They had come for me, sent by Mum. 'Oh hell,' I thought, 'home again.' But I was in for a shock.

We drove for a while in the wrong direction and pulled into a fortress-like building.

'Where the hell have you brought me?' I demanded.

'Newstead Girls' Home. You're too young for prison. Only fourteen, aren't you?'

'Prison!' I gulped.

They pushed me roughly inside and left me in the hands of a large, loudly-spoken woman. 'Right. Into the bathroom and everything off,' she barked at me.

'What do you mean?'

'Just what I said. Take your clothes off, girl.'

Inside I was cringing, but I tried to maintain a careless bravado.

A nurse came in and disinfected my whole body. Humiliation and anger were welling up inside me. She searched me from head to foot, presumably looking for drugs. I was given a uniform to wear and led to a cell-like room with one small barred window. The door clicked locked behind the nurse.

Nights and days melted into one long nightmare.

> *God, the walls are closing in on me. I can't see any daylight. I'm terrified. I've got to pull myself higher up those bars. Got to see daylight. I can't breathe. There's no air. I'm going to suffocate.*

I collapsed for about the tenth time on the floor beside the high little window. Utter despair engulfed me.

The routine was tightly regimented. I hated it. Hated all the staff. And most of all I hated my mother for sending me here. It was the final betrayal. After a while my emotions became numb. Something had snapped inside me.

> *I'm going to kill myself. All I want is to die. But I'm scared, terrified of what's on the other side when you die. What if it's worse? God, if you exist, why are you punishing me like this? This is hell already. Nothing could be worse.*

I'm going to commit suicide. I'll find a way. I'm not hanging around for people to hurt me any longer.

I began to hear voices. Sometimes it was all right, but often I was tormented out of my brain. During the long, usually sleepless nights, my mind was wracked with terror and conflict. 'Tomorrow's the day, Jodie. Watch for your chance. Cut your wrists. You'll be better off dead,' the voices would say. One long night I could bear it no longer. I knew I had to do something.

Morning crept stealthily into my cell and the winter sun lay in pale watery pools on the cold floor. Today I would do it.

Chapter Three

Cautiously I fingered the cover of the Bible on my locker. My shaking hand found dozens of valium tablets and sleeping pills, which I'd been saving for today. I had to move quickly before someone saw me. I put them all into my mouth at once and chewed them quickly. At last I would be able to sink into the oblivion of death.

*Will it really be oblivion? What if there **is** something on the other side? What if there **is** a place called hell? What if it's worse? No. It couldn't be worse. This is hell already, if there's a hell.*

I gritted my teeth and tried to act normally.

Soon I was dressed in my uniform, just like any other day. There was the breakfast bell. Already my head was swimming. No, I didn't want breakfast. No more food. The hard little bed felt surprisingly comfortable. Was I floating? Everything felt so soft and fluid. Except my mouth and nose. My mouth was getting drier and drier and I began to gasp for air and moisture. Darkness engulfed me and waves of strange dull terror swept over me as I listened to the harsh, distant sound of my own rasping breaths. I had thought it would be pleasant, sinking into oblivion. But instead a great swirling darkness was sucking me inside it and I couldn't breathe. I tried to scream, but no sound would come from my dehydrated throat.

It seemed as if no time had passed. Voices were talking in the darkness. Talking about me. I tried to move my hand to see if I was really alive, but it wouldn't work. My body seemed disconnected from me—a heavy useless weight.

'Poor kid, she's had a rough trot,' one of the staff was saying.

'How is she, doctor?'

'She'll be all right. She's only taken enough to knock herself out for a while. Could be a bit of liver damage. You'll have to keep a closer eye on her.'

'Silly little brat.' It was the matron's loud bark. 'She makes life hard for herself. And for us, I might add.'

Then I was drifting again and everything was muffled.

A few days later I was up and about. Immediately the merciless regime resumed. This time it was even worse. The staff watched my every movement. Even the other girls viewed me with caution or curiosity. I returned their glances with a sullen hostility. I went wearily, angrily, through the motions of life. If you could call it life. I should have guessed it would take more dope than that to kill me. Kathy and I had been smoking marijuana, taking valium and any other pills we could get, and drinking heavily since I was thirteen. My system was pretty used to it all already.

After three months I was released from the home. I went back to Mum and the boys. At least it was a roof over my head.

Dad was there occasionally, but he and Mum led separate lives. The only thing they had in common was a determination to make me 'keep the home rules'. Apart from that, they'd both given up on me. Neither of them tried to communicate with me at all.

I didn't return to school. After my rebellion and humiliation at my former school and the trauma of the girls' home, I couldn't face another institution. Fortunately, nobody tried to force me.

The tensions at home were unbearable. Jonothan pulled me aside one day. 'Listen, Sis, I can't handle this. I'm going to split.'

'You can't, Jono. Not yet, anyway. Dad will probably leave again soon. It'll probably be better then.' But it wasn't. It was worse.

The one consolation in my life, apart from Jono, was bikes. Before long, Jono caught my enthusiasm and was soon one of a bike gang.

One incident around this time stands out in sharp contrast to the painful turmoil surrounding it. When I was about fifteen Mum took the boys and me for a few weeks' holiday in Australia. Mum had a sister living in Queensland, near Maryborough, so we stayed with her and her family most of the time.

As soon as we walked through the door I had the strangest sensation. Something was different in this place. It was like stepping into a peaceful little pool of sunshine after being tossed around in a cold gale outside. My aunt was kind and seemed interested in me and the boys. She treated me like a real person, not just an object that was in the road.

After a few days, I discovered the reason for their different-ness. My aunt and uncle and their son John, who was about my age, were all Christians. Full-on, praise-the-Lord-type Christians. Religious freaks. I was disappointed. Disgusted, in fact. Yet I was strangely attracted to the feeling of peace and warmth emanating from them.

We returned to New Zealand, and I soon forgot about my relations, as I was whirled into the vortex of an emotional cyclone. Little did I realise how significant this soon-dismissed encounter had been.

Mum's bitterness and lack of communication became more than I could bear, so I left home, storming out in one of my rages, and went flatting with Kathy.

It was fun—for a while. We had plenty of parties and the bikers were in and out of the flat frequently. Then, one night when I was stoned out of my brain on a combination of marijuana, pills and alcohol, one of the guys beat me up badly.

When I awoke the next morning, I was sore all over. I dragged myself to the bathroom and looked in the mirror. A black eye. An ugly bruise on my cheek. Perhaps Kathy could get something from the chemist to help the pain in my head. I reached for my purse. It was empty.

'Hell, Kathy!' I screamed, 'I've been ripped off. All my money's gone.'

My short angry burst of energy drained quickly and left me limp and depressed. Aching. Defeated, I went back home.

This pattern continued for about a year. I would go home, stay there till I couldn't handle it any longer, then go flatting. Each time I'd get beaten up or my money stolen and I'd have to return home.

Keith had faded into the background. He was really messed up from heroin. By the time I was fifteen, I was sleeping around indiscriminately.

One of my bouts of living at home was more

traumatic than usual. Mum and Dad were officially separated then, and debt collectors came around with an eviction notice. We packed up and went to stay with relatives. Theirs was a small house and we all slept on their loungeroom floor. For the first few days, there had been a sort of bond between us. Even the hostility between Mum and me disappeared briefly, as were all united in our common troubles. But with our living in such cramped quarters, the tensions soon resurfaced with a vengeance.

One day the boys pulled me aside. 'Heh, Jode, what is it with Dad, anyway?' asked Roger.

'What do you mean?' I replied blankly.

'The kids at school are all saying he's gay.' Roger sounded distressed.

The realisation fell into place quickly. Of course. That explained a lot. Memories of his weird friends and that ghastly weekend party flashed through my mind. It was true. How humiliating.

The divorce came through and Mum started working towards getting another house. By this time I was sixteen and almost an alcoholic. I needed drink to soften the hard edges of the reality that was my life. And I needed more and more of it.

Then I met Bob. I was standing by myself in a smoky corner at a party when he first came up to me. Soon we were deep in conversation. He wanted to know all about me. That was unusual. Nobody except Jonothan had shown any real interest in me as a person for years. I hardly knew what to say.

'What's with the jeans and shirt bit? Trying to be one of the guys?' he asked.

My defences were up immediately. 'Why not?' I asked almost angrily. 'Guys get a better deal in life than girls.'

He looked at me strangely, not understanding my sudden hostility. 'I'll bet you're a real pretty chick when you're done up.'

Pretty! I never thought much about my appearance these days, except to glare resentfully at my reflection in the mirror. With my short, straight, brown hair and hazel eyes I looked, and felt, boyish.

Being unused to so much attention, I became totally infatuated with Bob. Soon we were living together in a small, shabby flat.

It was a tempestuous relationship. The sensitive, caring Bob who had won my affections disappeared every time he drank. An angry, aggressive Bob would replace him. His drinking bouts were frequent, and he bashed me badly several times.

I was a mess. Like Bob, I drank heavily. And I was addicted to barbiturates. Concerned about my violent rages and my addictions, Bob tried to persuade me to see a psychiatrist.

'Man, you've got to be joking,' I retorted angrily. 'A bloody shrink. Fat lot of good they do.'

So Bob tried to 'beat me into shape' himself. I was confused. I loved Bob with a slavish adoration, knowing his concern for me was genuine. But when he was drinking—or when my rages took over—we fought violently, hurling both words and fists at each other.

Sometimes my anger and confusion, and the deep well of despair underneath it all, would overwhelm me. Several times I overdosed on barbiturates, trying to kill myself. I would land in hospital, unconscious, and remain unconscious for about eight hours. But I always came out the other end.

Frustrated with my abortive attempts at suicide with pills, one day, in a fit of rage, I grabbed a sharp knife and slashed my wrists. Bob came in, grabbed me and took me, dripping blood everywhere, up to the hospital.

I became pregnant. Although I was only eighteen and in a mess physically and emotionally, I felt almost glad. Maybe a baby would sort everything out. A baby would need me and belong to me. Something almost like happiness flickered through me. But then, at times, I'd scream and throw things at the walls in a confused agony of frustration at my situation.

A few months later, Bob and I were driving to the coast to visit friends. We were cruising along at a good speed, enjoying the fresh country air. Suddenly a car appeared in front of us from a side lane. He didn't stop. Bob screeched the brakes and I screamed. Everything whirled before my eyes and there was a hideous metallic crash and the sound of breaking glass. Soon I was in hospital again.

I've lost the baby. I know I have. Nobody's game to tell me. Maybe they think I'm still unconscious. I wonder if it was a boy or a girl. It's gone now. I'm not going to be a mother after all. My whole body's aching. All that for nothing. God, if you're there, why couldn't you have let me die?

Before long another baby was on the way. I decided not to tell Bob for a while. He'd had a few negative reactions about my first pregnancy. One night he was drunk and beat me savagely. I collapsed in pain. Another miscarriage.

Bob had had as much as he could take. A woman who threw crazy fits of anger and even beat *him* up, my addictions and my many moods, pregnancies and now two miscarriages. Things were going from bad to worse. So he left me.

He was all I'd lived for for three years. Now he was gone. I was a physical wreck—pathetically skinny, still feeling weak and ill; my hair which I'd grown long to please Bob, thin and stringy.

There was still Jonothan. I would keep living for him. Dear Jono, who cared enough to try so hard to stop my drinking and drug abuse. But

Jono, too, was in trouble with the cops for drug using and he was edgy at times.

There was no real 'home' to go to. Just a house that Mum was working to pay off. Dad was gone and Mum was miserable and bitter. We used Mum and her house, arriving at any hour of the day or night and leaving when we felt like it. The rough guys I mixed with would turn up at all hours demanding to see me.

I didn't care about any of the guys. They were just objects I used. When Bob left, I wiped men. Except Jono. My life became a self-destructive whirlpool of alcohol and drugs. I drank myself into oblivion night and day. Nothing mattered any more.

I couldn't hold down a job. In the past three years I'd gone from being a well-groomed receptionist to an unkempt factory worker. For a while I tried to pretend everything was okay. Something would work out, surely. I continued to mix with the bikers and drank heavily with them, and slept with anyone I could. Pretended to be cool.

I'm laughing on the outside, but on the inside I'm crying. Nobody knows who I am. Nobody except Jonothan. If anything happened to Jono, I'd die. When he came off his bike the other day, I thought, 'I'd be too terrified to be alive without Jono.' Life's empty. What's it all about, anyway? I'm so angry most of the time, I feel like killing someone.

Or myself. Nobody understands except Jonothan, and he must get sick of me. He must be ashamed to be my brother, sometimes. What's it like to have the local whore as your sister, I wonder. What's it like being the local whore? I don't know. Can't think clearly. But I'm lonely. So lonely I want to die.

Then I met Ray and moved in with him. He was in and out of gaol on burglary charges. But Jonothan liked him. Said he was a good guy. That was high praise from Jono. Jono, who saw through everyone's facades. So I stayed with Ray when he wasn't in gaol.

Much to my delight, Jono was still in a bike gang. I'd feel so proud to be his sister as I saw him riding past in all his leather gear. Everyone admired Jonothan.

One evening, when I was home alone preparing tea, he appeared at the door. 'Sis, I want to talk to you.'

My heart sank at the serious, almost stern, tone in his voice. 'What?'

'Jodie, you've got to stop all this. Ray's okay. You want to stick with him. Stop going off with the other guys when Ray's in prison. And stop dropping all those pills. And the booze too. Have a bit of respect for yourself.'

'Respect!' I retorted. 'Why the hell should I? Nobody else ever respected me.'

'I do,' said Jonothan quietly. He looked at me

intently. 'Sis, you're class. Stop acting like the local whore.'

I choked back a sob. Tears streamed down my face despite my efforts to stop them. 'Everything's a mess,' I sobbed. 'I wouldn't know where to start trying to be different. It's too late to change myself, anyway.'

'No, it's not.' Jonothan was unyielding. 'Do it for me, Sis. And for yourself.' He changed the subject and shared bits of local bike news for a while, then left.

Maybe he's right. He really believes in me. Nobody else ever did. Maybe I could change. Not go really straight—I couldn't handle that. But perhaps I could pull myself together a bit more. Jono would be so proud of me.

A few days later I was out with Ray. When I came home there was a note from Jono on the bench. 'I'll be back soon,' it read. 'Great,' I thought, 'he still hasn't given up on me.'

But 'soon' never came. Jonothan never came back. That was the day he was killed. It was the beginning of the walking death in which I lived till I found myself on a plane heading for Sydney.

Chapter Four

The plane circled the huge city of Sydney. Never had I seen houses so tightly packed together. In the middle was a blue expanse of water with inlets radiating in all directions. Sydney Harbour. The plane swooped down and we were racing along the runway of Mascot Airport.

Pete's friends, New Zealanders, met us at the airport. They seemed a nice friendly group. 'We'll put you up till you find somewhere to live,' they assured us both. Somewhere to live. I hadn't even thought about it.

They were all using 'smack' (heroin).

'Come on, sweetheart,' said long-haired Graham. 'Try it. What've you got to lose.'

'Nothing,' I said dully.

So I started using smack. At first it seemed like heaven after the torment of real life. We went out stoned out of our brains and walked around Kings Cross. Man, this place was really alive! Crazy-looking characters of all kinds appeared and then disappeared into the crowd. There were lots of people of different nationalities, too. I enjoyed the cosmopolitan atmosphere of the Cross.

After a few days, Pete and his friends and I went up to the Gold Coast to visit a few more New Zealanders. Queensland. That was where my cousin, John, lived. He was working in Brisbane now.

'Want to go and check him out, Jodie?' asked Pete.

'No way,' I almost snapped back. 'He's a weirdo—a religious freak. Says he's a Christian.'

'Oh,' Pete laughed understandingly.

Pete wanted to stay on the Coast for a while. He tried to persuade me to stay with him, but I was sick of him and was keen to get back to Sydney. So he gave me fifty dollars and I headed off without him.

Reality started to hit me when I found myself at Central Station in Sydney. People were rushing in all directions. I was alone. I had no money. No job. Nobody here knew me. I had nowhere to live.

At least the people back home knew me, even if they couldn't handle me. Man, I must be crazy. What am I going to do? What does it matter, anyway? I may as well die here as anywhere else. I don't want to live without Jonothan. Oh, Jonothan, where are you now? I wonder if he's still there somewhere. And if he knows what I'm thinking.

I found my way through the maze of the city to the flat where Pete's friends were living. 'Please, let me stay for awhile,' I begged.

They looked at me reluctantly. 'Okay. But only for two nights. You'll have to find a place of your own.'

So that night I tasted smack again. It seemed wonderful—the euphoric sense of leaving all my problems behind me just drifting. Nothing mattered any more.

True to their word, the guys insisted I leave after two days. I had one last hope: the address of some other people I'd known in New Zealand. I found their place and banged frantically on the door.

The girl who opened the door looked at me in angry dismay. 'What the hell are you doing here?' was her greeting.

'Please, let me stay with you. Just for a week. I've got no money. I've got to find a job. Jonothan's dead. He came off his bike. *Please* let me stay.'

Anne was reluctant. She knew my reputation from New Zealand and didn't want anything to do with me. But she and her friends were sorry about Jonothan. Eventually they agreed. I could stay for a week.

During that week I walked the streets of Glebe and the outer city area looking for work. Ragged and unkempt in my old jeans, I went from shop to shop, restaurant to restaurant, begging for work. After four days I felt desperate. My week was running out and still no job.

At last a restaurant near Glebe agreed to employ me as a kitchen hand. They gave me a bag of old clothes to wear to work. It was a sixty-hour week, so I received a reasonable wage.

I searched *The Sydney Morning Herald* and answered an advertisement: *Flatmate Wanted*. It was in Glebe. Ideal.

There were several guys and girls living in the flat. They were all gay. It didn't worry me. I no longer valued my life, so I didn't care who I mixed with.

Actually, they were a likeable group of people. I understood them because of having watched my father's behaviour. Although I still felt disgusted with my father, I felt a sort of affinity with these guys. They were social outcasts, as I had become. And yet, they were real people with real feelings.

I baulked at getting involved in an actual relationship with any of them, but enjoyed going to their clubs with them. I enjoyed the strange feeling of belonging as we would enter what looked like a warehouse or any old building, to find a dimly-lit interior with only a select group allowed to go there—the homosexuals. Many of them were drug dealers too, so I managed to get smack and other dope cheaply.

The biggest external hassle in my life then was my job. Joe, the owner, would greet me with his greasy smile as I arrived. 'Ah, you are four minutes late today, Jodie. Always late. Never on time. You must work hard to make up for it.'

So I'd sweat away over the filthy pots and pans for ten hours a day, six days a week. By the end of each day I was exhausted. 'Not much flesh on you,' Joe would remark, pinching my arm. 'We must fatten you up.' Every time he touched me I recoiled in revulsion.

My flatmates thought I was crazy to put up with the job. They were all earning better money with less effort. One was a topless barmaid in a pub in Pyrmont. One was a stripper. A few of them were dealers.

'Jodie, there's a job going at the pub,' Kelly, the topless barmaid, greeted me one day. 'Why don't you try for it? I'll put in a word for you.'

I got the job. The money was good. The customers were rough. Workers from the docks, the ships and the toughest bike gangs in Sydney would come in. Their parties were wild and I enjoyed them. Sniffing cocaine was something new and I loved it. Plenty of speed was available and I lived on it. It helped to lift my emotions above the sordid situation I was in. Tough-looking bikers would saunter into the bar and look me up and down before ordering a drink.

I'm not really that kind of girl. Not the kind of slut they think I am. Jonothan always said I had class. I'm not like these other chicks. I'm only doing it for the money. I'll soon be out of it. But I've got to survive in this place and make enough for dope as well. This isn't really who I am. If only one person really loved me, I'd get out of this place. Give it all up. Just one person. But nobody cares.

Gradually the scene gripped me. I was free. Free of my family's disapproval. I was an adult now. No-one could ever tell me what to do again. I could go anywhere, do anything. Endless nebulous exciting possibilities paraded through my mind. Free. With the help of various drugs, I was free even of my own limitations. Life had no boundaries. Like an excited child taking sweets from a stranger, I began running faster and faster towards the steel prison door that was labelled *Freedom*.

I realised my body could earn me money. There had been plenty of offers but I'd always refused them. That would be the last step. No, I wouldn't let myself sink that low.

Then I met up with Tom, who had sold me smack before. He gave me a couple of free tastes. It seemed like bliss; that incredible feeling of well-being and the sense of all my problems being removed from me. From that time on, I began to crave heroin obsessively. I was willing to pay anything for it now. Anything and everything.

Chapter Five

A room became vacant at another pub near the one where I worked, so I moved there. My life became an endless party—using dope, partying, stoned out of my brain, working in the pub. My new friends were a way-out crowd; an assortment of crims, dealers, sailors, bikers, anyone. Anyone tough, that is.

One day I walked into the bar to work and found Kelly had left. She'd finally decided to join several others who'd left to work as prostitutes instead. The money was so much better and they needed it to support their drug habits. A peculiar feeling of desolation crept over me. The bar seemed ugly and lonely without her.

Roxanne, a tough, red-headed girl who had

worked on the streets before coming to the pub, began to befriend me. She was a warm, friendly, down-to-earth girl and I enjoyed her matter-of-fact approach to life. There were plenty of laughs when Roxanne was around.

'Jodie,' she came up to me one day, 'I'm going back to work on the streets. The money's so much better.'

My heart sank. 'What's it like, Roxy?' I asked. 'I mean, it must be awful selling your body.'

'Oh, it's not too bad,' she replied vaguely. 'Specially if you're stoned. You don't even think about it then. You should try it Jodie . . . for the money.'

She had hit the nail on the head. I needed money badly. My heroin habit was starting to cost more than my barmaid's wages. I would give it a try. Just once or twice, for the money. I'd keep my job at the bar as well.

The first time I sold myself I cried the whole time. I hated it, everything about it. Hated my fat, greasy client. Hated myself. But when I saw that money in my hand, I was elated. I went straight out that night and got a fix; blew all my money on it.

Soon I was longing for more heroin. I could think of nothing else. So I sold myself again . . . and again and again and again. After a while, I didn't care any more. I'd lost any remaining self-respect. I just lived for money to get dope. Soon I left my barmaid's job.

It's okay. Lots of chicks are doing it. Decent chicks like Roxy. These men aren't using me. I'm the one using them. Sucking their money out of them. I'm winning in this game.

The face that looked back at me from the mirror became harder and harder. Once I caught sight of my reflection and nearly freaked. What was happening to me? How had I become that skinny, hard-faced girl with the cold, glassy eyes? So I had another fix and then nothing mattered anymore. I was free. Floating.

Roxy and I took a flat together. A small dingy flat in a large old building at Kings Cross. 'Potts Point,' the address said. It sounded like a nice place, maybe even posh. But it was only a minute's walk from the heart of the Cross and I soon began to realise there was nothing nice or posh about Kings Cross. Not for me, anyway. It was a hard, ugly place.

Roxy had a seven-year-old son who lived with us. Robbie, she called him. Robbie would pick up Roxy out of her own vomit and try to wake her when she'd overdosed, which happened several times.

I used to pick Dad up when he came home drunk, just like Robbie does. Where's Dad now, I wonder? What would he think of me? Probably wouldn't care. Mum would hate my guts for it. But she never loved me anyway. Jono would've cared. He would've been angry and tried to get me out of it. But I wouldn't be doing it if Jono were alive. He cared about me. Hell, I can't afford to think like this. I need another fix.

Robbie's presence irritated me. I was growing quite attached to Roxanne. She was the only real friend I had. I resented Robbie's presence and his intrusion into our relationship.

Sometimes I would look at Roxy and wonder how on earth we had become so friendly. She stood for everything I hated about my lifestyle. Her brilliantly dyed red hair, stark white face with vividly reddened cheeks and scarlet lips made her look like what she was—a prostitute. Her sense of humour had deteriorated as she became harder and more bitter. It was now coarse, accompanied by a harsh, brittle laugh. But her eyes never laughed now. They just stared at me; two dull brown (or were they black?) pools with small pin-point pupils. When she started joking, I felt horribly alone. Isolated in my own world where nothing was funny any more unless I was even more stoned than usual. But Roxy and I had worked quite happily in the pub together, and now we worked the streets together. We shared our lifestyle, our anxieties, our desperations, our triumphs.

And Roxy was tough. Tougher than I was. She'd been working the streets for years. She was in her early thirties while I was only twenty-two. Roxy knew the Cross and its underworld like the back of her hand and, in a funny way, I idolised her.

She would disappear for days on end, working on ships. I hated this. Hated being left alone in that God-forsaken dump of a flat. And having no shoulder to cry on when I came home after a night's work. No-one to get stoned with. The scene was frightening when I was alone. And she always left the kid there.

One weekend we shifted flats again to another part of the Cross. On the Saturday night, Roxy went to a party. She wasn't back still on Sunday afternoon. Typical. Partying on, probably stoned out of her brain. Maybe she'd gone to work on a ship, even. Great. That left me with Robbie, and tomorrow he had to start at a new school because of our changed address. The new flat was more than walking distance from his old school.

Monday morning came. The early sunlight slunk through the crack between the curtains in a pale, furtive shaft that hurt my eyes. I buried my face in the pillow.

Robbie was shaking me. 'Wake up, Jodie, we've got to go to my new school,' his insistent voice repeated. I was aching from head to foot after three hours' sleep. Somehow I stumbled out of bed, dressed and ran a comb through my hair.

It must have been too long since I'd had a fix, because suddenly it was there again. Blinding white-hot fury surged through me. 'Shut up, you brat,' I shouted at Robbie. 'I hate you. I've had you. You're too much trouble. Always in the way. Always wanting "Mummy". Well Mummy's too damn busy to care. Look what you're doing to me, getting me out of bed after three hours' sleep. I had to work last night. *You* didn't.'

The rage drained out of me and I ran and got another fix. But not before I'd noticed Robbie's eyes. They could have been beautiful eyes, big and green, but they weren't beautiful. There was something wrong. Two small tears ran down Robbie's pale, thin little cheeks. Hell, was the kid going to bawl? But then I noticed that I was not looking into the eyes of a kid of seven at all. They were the eyes of an adult—a street-hardened adult like Roxy or me. I realised that Robbie, at the age of seven, understood everything that was going on and he wasn't really a child at all. He probably never had been. The impression was to stay with me for years. Then I felt the blissful prick of the needle in my arm and Robbie didn't matter.

Roxanne reappeared on Tuesday. I was lonely and depressed by then and Robbie was agitated and aggressive. He ran up to her and grabbed her arm. 'Where've you been, Mummy, where've you been? I've been really naughty.' Roxy grabbed him and gave him a hiding, then pushed him away. A fleeting look of triumph crossed his face, then he retreated into feeling hurt.

This became a pattern. Roxy would disappear

and leave me, feeling lonely and insecure, to look after Robbie. Four times I had to take him to new schools, as we moved flats so often, always on the run from some creep.

One bleak, gusty, July day Roxy returned after one of her jaunts. I was tired and edgy. Robbie had been awkward and disobedient but, more than anything, I simply resented his presence. Having to look after someone else's kid. And having that kid take so large a place in the affections of my only friend. Perhaps, in a strange sort of way, I was jealous of him.

Anyway, Roxy walked in. Or rather, flew in. She was really flying high on dope and pleased with herself for having earned more money than usual.

Usually I was so relieved to have her back home that I went along with whatever she suggested, joined sympathetically in her current mood. This time was different. Somewhere inside myself, under the layers of hardness and heroin, I was at screaming point. Being dumped with Robbie again had tried me to my wits' end, and I felt a curious sense of betrayal. Roxy wasn't really playing the game by the rules. (Roxy probably didn't have any 'rules', after being street-hardened and unscrupulous for years, but I still had some. Strictly of my own choosing, of course.)

The clock was ticking loudly behind me. Ticking away the minutes till Robbie came home from school. One of the filthy orange curtains billowed as a gust of icy wind came through the crack between the windows. I shivered and gritted my teeth.

'Shut up for a minute and listen to me,' I interrupted Roxy's chatter as she recounted her exploits.

'What's with you?' Roxy asked, surprised.

The words tumbled out. Even though the idea had been forming inside me for awhile, I was almost shocked as it came spilling out of me.

'Robbie's got to go. I can't handle him any longer. Wake up to yourself. Roxanne, you can't look after him and I can't either. You're going to have to get rid of him.'

'What do you mean "get rid of him"?'

'Put him in a home. A welfare home.'

Roxanne blanched. She wasn't flying any longer, but sitting deflated and defeated, on the shabby sofa.

'No way,' she said in a flat voice.

Anger welled up inside me. 'Don't be so damned selfish,' I screamed at her. 'You can't keep the kid if you're going to keep splitting the scene and leaving him with me. I'm sick of having your garbage dumped on me. If you want to keep him, maybe you'd better give up work. But you can't. You know you can't. You're trapped in it like I am to get the money for dope.'

Roxanne was growing whiter all the time. I wondered if she was going to pass out. Finally she muttered in a low, dull voice that sounded almost as if she didn't care, 'Okay, he can go.'

Roxy knew she was beaten. And I saw, for a brief glimpse, that she was beaten not by me but by life. Tough, triumphant Roxy. I could hardly bear it. Quickly I closed my mind to her suffering, and to my own.

The next day we took Robbie to a welfare home. Roxy couldn't tell Robbie it was permanent. As she waved goodbye to him she called in a brittle voice, 'I'll be back to get you in a week, Robbie.'

'In time for my birthday?' Robbie asked.

'Yes,' lied Roxy, swallowing, 'in time for your birthday.' But she never went back. The high metal gates clanged shut behind us with a harsh finality.

Once I was put in a home. I remember the gates shutting behind me. I was so lonely and scared. And so angry with my parents. Robbie will feel like I felt. If he's got any feelings left. Now it's me helping to lock a kid away in a home. I don't even feel sorry for him. I don't feel anything. I hardly know who I am any more.

As we walked back to the flat, the cold July wind whipped off the harbour and stung our faces. I stepped over somebody's spilt garbage at the foot of the steps and pushed open the heavy old door. Our feet echoed coldly in the emptiness of the dark hallway.

Chapter Six

Days melted into weeks, melted into months with the sinister, inescapable quality of a nightmare. Nothing made sense. Life was agony. And yet heroin was bliss.

I loved heroin, and hated it. Hated it because I knew it was killing me. Sapping the strength from my body, the flesh from my bones. We knew several people who had died from heroin. Usually it was an overdose and nobody ever knew if it was suicide, murder or just an accident. But we were all dying gradually as our livers and kidneys cracked up from prolonged drug and alcohol abuse.

I got more and more into prostitution. I

needed the money. My 'habit' cost me three hundred dollars a fix now.

I thought I was used to selling myself and that I didn't care. But I did really. I never managed inwardly to become the tough prostitute I was on the outside. Nearly every night after work I'd feel so filthy I'd get into the shower clothes and all. For hours, often, I'd stand there under the streaming water gradually peeling off my clothes and washing myself. Finally disinfecting myself from head to foot. Crying. Choking back the constant desire to vomit.

One of my hated enemies was the mirror in the bedroom. Without it, I could almost forget who I was. Forget I existed, even, floating on a sea of heroin. I'd stand in front of the mirror and stare at myself. Tears of rage and frustration would fill my eyes and I'd scream at the reflection, 'I hate you, hate you, hate you.'

*Who **is** this hard-faced skinny woman staring out of the mirror at me? She's betrayed me. Made me sell myself till there's no 'me' left. No, Roxy's betrayed me. It was her idea. No, it was Jonothan. Why did you die and leave me alone in this torture, Jono?'*

My only comfort and support came from my friendship with Roxanne. Like most prostitutes, Roxy had become a lesbian. She felt only revulsion and contempt for men, now. They were simply her source of income. I was beginning to feel the same revulsion.

Kelly, who had first led me into topless barmaiding and then led the way into prostitution, was flatting with a small, thin girl called Shana. Shana had straight black hair almost to her waist and looked quite startling—all well-made-up eyes and hair. I noticed her hair was looking thin and lanky lately. She and Kelly had been on smack longer than I had. I guessed it was destroying them.

I'd maintained a sort of friendship with these girls and with two of the other street-workers, Chris and Liz. Not that any of my friendships were very real. Nobody trusted anyone else in that scene.

On a cold, blustery August night when I was at work, the phone rang. Chris, at the desk, took the call. It was a customer. The one with Shana. Chris's forehead creased, as it always did when there was bad news. The customer was almost shouting into the phone in a mixture of anger and guilt. 'She died on me,' he choked out in a shaky voice. Chris relayed it to me.

So Shana was dead. Small, skinny Shana with the hair many of us envied.

'What do we do?' I asked, feeling nothing like grief and yet strangely shattered.

'Nothing.' Chris's forehead creased again. 'We can't go and get her or anything. We don't want to get dragged into it.'

So that was that. All night, even while I

worked, I couldn't rid myself of the image of Shana lying, dead, her cold white face framed by black hair strewn across a pillow. Dead and alone.

Kelly was distraught and used more heroin to get through it. Only a few weeks later we received a similar call. This time Kelly was dead.

Maybe it'll be my turn next. We're all dying in this place. I'd rather be dead but I'm still scared. Where's Kelly now? And Shana? Do they still exist somewhere? What's life all about? What's the point in it all? If only death was really the end and I could be sure about it.

Life was turning into an ugly charade. It all seemed a bit unreal, like a hideous horror film. With the smack and other dope I used, I felt strangely detached from it all. I was in it, going through the motions of everything, yet I was not really a part of it.

Our lifestyle had become bizarre. Roxy and I still shared a flat, but usually several other people would be staying with us. They were a grotesque array of characters—dealers, crims, people on the run from the police, drag queens, gays, you name it. We had become like a travelling circus. I didn't know any normal people any more.

I still went with bike gangs; the toughest ones in Sydney. I knew if I crossed them they'd blow me off the face of the earth.

A disturbing sense of unreality nagged at me. I craved something real. A real relationship with real people. Suddenly I knew what I wanted to do. I had a bit of money put aside. I'd invite Mum and Roger over from New Zealand for a few weeks holiday. Family, real, live, normal people who knew who I really was. Perhaps they would even love me now.

Of course, I couldn't let them know about my work. Or my drug habit. I couldn't bear them to despise me. So I organised an elaborate game, like stage-managing a major production. I took a small flat of my own, away from my weird-looking 'friends'. Carefully, I persuaded my friends to take part in my grand performance by pretending to be normal people with normal jobs.

I met Mum and Roger at the airport. Mum had aged a lot in the past three years. Her hair was almost grey and her skin looked tired. I choked back the familiar mixture of emotions at seeing her: anger, hurt and love (if you could call it love). Then I was overwhelmed with sheer gladness at having them there. I was a real person with a real family. I laughed at Roger's newly grown-up image, as he fingered his beard proudly. He was eighteen now, and towered over me.

'Jodie.' Mum's voice was tired but happy. 'Well, you look real good. Got some decent clothes for a change. I never thought you'd get yourself together so well.'

I swallowed back an angry retort. Nothing was going to spoil this time for me.

Mum continued, 'You could do with a bit of weight on, though. Are you eating properly?'

'Yes, when I have time,' I lied with a laugh. 'Life's pretty hectic in Sydney. Wait till you meet my friends. I'm fat compared with Roxy.'

Mum grunted disapprovingly, but I could see a reluctant admiration glimmering in her eyes. I'd finally made it with her, I thought, even if I'd had to fool her to do it.

I loved having them there. And I quite enjoyed keeping up the pretence of normality, despite a few tense moments when someone dropped a wrong word. There were plenty of laughs. And Mum really was sucked in.

Roger decided to stay on in Sydney after Mum left. I was delighted but apprehensive. It would be so good to have someone there who cared about me, someone I could trust. But how long could I keep up this elaborate facade? How long before I, or one of the others, blew it?

I hesitated as Roger asked if he could stay on in the flat with me. 'Come on, Jode,' he urged. 'It's been great seeing you. I really dig some of your friends, too. It's boring back home.'

The idea of having 'family', real, live, normal family, there with me was too good to knock back. 'Okay, Roger,' I grinned, 'but you'll have to behave yourself.'

'Who's talking?' he retorted.

So Roger settled in with me. He slept in the

lounge and I kept all my smack and syringes and stuff in the bedroom. I tried desperately to keep up the pretence, making sure I always had a fix before I was really hanging out, and slipping off to work with an overcoat over my clothes.

One night I came home more tired than usual. When I dragged myself out for a cup of coffee in the morning, Roger eyed me suspiciously. My hands were shaking.

'What's going on, Jodie?' he demanded.

'What do you mean?'

'Come on, now,' he said sarcastically. 'How much longer do you expect me to swallow your fairytales about "going straight"? There's something weird going on in this place.'

'Look, it's nothing much,' I said desperately. 'Roger, you wouldn't understand. You've just left school. I don't want to talk about it. Just leave me in peace. Everything's okay.'

'Is it? You could've fooled me,' he said in a strangely hollow voice. 'Whatever it is you and your friends are into, I don't like it. You're always lying. The whole damn lot of you look sick half the time. And I don't trust that guy, Tom. I always get the feeling he's out to get me, or trying to suck me into something.'

I suppressed a shudder as I thought of Tom's steely eyes. 'Stay away from Tom,' I snapped.

'I thought you said he was your friend,' said Roger.

I sighed and walked away.

That evening Roxy came over and Roger was

talking to her when I emerged from the shower. There was something almost sinister about her as she sat hunched on the sofa, leaning conspiratorially towards Roger, her red hair glinting in the lamplight.

'He knows,' she said calmly. 'He already guessed part of it, so I told him the rest.'

I swore at her.

'Okay, Roger,' I sighed. And I told him the whole story from my point of view.

He cracked. Cracked right up and cried and cried.

This can't be happening. My only remaining brother. He won't trust me any more. I feel so dirty. He'll think I'm filth. Damn Roxy, why couldn't she keep her mouth shut? I guess he had to find out. Hell, it's freaked him right out.

When Roger's initial outburst had died down, he said in a choked voice, 'Jodie, I want you to get off that stuff.'

'I can't,' I screamed at him. 'Do you think I like being a junkie? Do you think I enjoy having to poke needles in my arm just to keep going?'

'You don't need it. I don't believe it. You've been sucked in by Tom and his mates.'

'Shut up!' I said fiercely. 'Look, I'll try to give it up for you. I'll really try.'

But I couldn't. As soon as the smack started wearing off, all I could think of was the next fix.

I tried to wait longer before I had it, but soon my whole being was obsessed with a craving that was bigger than I was. With shaky hands, I grabbed a needle again.

I'm trapped. Trapped in a cage called heroin. The bars of the cage are like steel spikes through every muscle in my body. It's killing me. And yet I love it. Can't handle selling myself much longer, though. Night after night after night selling my body. One day, I'll make enough money to get out of all this. And I'll find a guy who'll support me. I'll still be able to have mountains of dope. I'll die floating through a sea of dope. There's no other way out of this cage.

Seeing my abortive, half-hearted attempts to kick the habit, Roger gradually lost respect for me. Finally, he just didn't care about me at all. And he was the only glimmer of hope I'd had in that nightmarish place.

He was changing, too. The 'glamorous' scene had reached out its tentacles and sucked him right in. It started with Roxanne. He fell for her and even lived with her for a while. My own brother, my young brother. Then he became involved in the camp scene through my weird friends—the gays, the drag queens, the transvestites, the real 'working scene' of the Cross. Then it was dope, but not smack. He was back living with me by then. I still sort of liked having him there, although we were really just using each other.

When I first saw him smoking dope, I freaked. 'If I ever find you've stuck a needle into your arm, I'll kill you,' I spat at him.

He looked at me, bewildered by my outburst.

'Yeah, okay,' I sighed, 'so I'm a junkie and all my friends are junkies, and it's killing us. But I'm not going to stand by and watch my own brother destroy himself like that. You'd be better off dead before you started.'

Roger shook his head. 'You sure are screwed up, Sis,' he said. 'If that's what smack does for you, you can have it. I want to get out of this place in one piece, when I leave.'

After a few weeks, I moved back in with Roxy and left Roger to entertain his camp friends. I was lonely. But Roxy was so often out all night or away for days on end. I'd come home from work and walk apprehensively down the cold dark hallway, hoping to avoid Big Bob, our landlord, who knew what we were doing. And desperately hoping to find Roxy home . . . someone to talk to and care about after the ugliness of work.

If Roxy was out, I'd lie in bed for hours crying from sheer loneliness. Terrified at the emptiness of life. What *was* it all about?

There's something missing in my life. Something's wrong. I feel as if I'm searching desperately for something and I don't even know what I'm searching for. Maybe it's happiness. Or love. I don't know. I've tried everything I know to kill the emptiness inside of me. Men, dope, everything. Nothing satisfies me. I still feel hollow. Frighteningly hollow. There's still something missing. Something important. Perhaps if I ever found it, I'd know what life was all about and what the point was in it all.

I encountered all sorts of freaks when I worked on the streets. Really kinky guys. I was terrified of them. Terrified they'd snap and turn on me and kill me. Some of them started following me around. I dreaded the thought of being followed home at night.

One night I arrived home to an empty flat. The silence was unnerving. Suddenly I heard a tap at the window. It was one of the freaks I'd seen that night. He'd followed me. A wave of panic swept over me. I grabbed the carving knife, went to the window and desperately plunged towards him. He took off. The next day I moved to an upstairs flat in the building and had special locks put on the doors and windows.

I was feeling sicker each day and getting so tired I found work almost unbearable.

'You'd better see a doctor, Jodie,' Roxy said. It was one of her more relaxed days and she seemed concerned for me.

I dragged myself off to the Cross's doctor, the

one who had a stream of junkies coming through his doors every day.

He looked at me sternly, then sighed with resignation. 'Hepatitis,' he said. 'Your liver's cracked up.'

It wasn't surprising. I'd been using any old needles I could lay my hands on lately, even rusty ones.

'Take a week or two off, and get some rest,' he said.

I swallowed a bitter laugh. Then I realised I'd managed to save a bit of money. It was nearly Christmas. That's what I'd do, go home to New Zealand for Christmas. I'd be okay after a break. I'd get my act together and then come back again.

Chapter Seven

Home wasn't home any more. It had changed and I'd changed. Not that I'd ever thought of it as the ultimate happy home—to put it mildly. I didn't even feel like me any more for the first week or so.

Christmas came and went with some superficial celebrations and gifts, but it didn't touch me. I just wasn't fully there on the inside. Strange, because I'd been really homesick at times. Maybe my memory had deceived me. One night in Sydney I'd been so desperately lonely that I'd rung Mum just to hear the sound of her voice. I was so lonely I'd clung to the phone and bawled my eyes out. 'What's wrong?' Mum had asked. 'Just . . . homesick,' I had gulped.

Now I was here and the loneliness was right here with me. My mind wandered over the events before I'd left. Roger wanting money from me now, just like everyone else. Roger wanting to return to New Zealand, but having no money. 'No way, you're on your own now,' I'd said, hardening myself to his needs. I was sick of being used. It seemed to be just Jodie against the world now.

Funny all the things that wandered through my mind now that I was away from it all. Roxanne's white face as she walked away from Robbie at the welfare home. That creepy guy at my window. Shana and Kelly, dead. And the endless, agonising nights alone at home when Roxy was out. And Jonothan. Always Jonothan.

After drifting aimlessly through a few more days, I realised I was feeling sicker. My hepatitis flared up instead of getting better and I became so sick I couldn't get off the bed. My liver really had cracked up.

I freaked as I lay there assessing my situation. I'd carefully smuggled in enough smack for two weeks. I'd already been here for ten days and I could hardly move, let alone go back to Sydney to work. I would have to ration out my remaining heroin carefully and just make do with less.

Days turned into weeks and still I was sick.

Man, I'm going off my brain, hanging out for a fix. My supply's nearly finished already. This is agony. I must have been crazy to come home. Sydney's where I belong.

My supply ran out and I went into withdrawal. I tried to hide the symptoms from my mother, hoping she'd think it was part of the hepatitis. But when my muscles and my whole insides started cramping up in agony, it was almost unbearable. The only things that helped me to cope with it were the barbiturates I'd obtained from the local doctor. I realised my withdrawal was much milder than most because of the barbs. I'd seen people twisted in pain, vomiting blood, from heroin withdrawal.

Gradually I recovered from hepatitis and by that time I'd dried out from smack. I could hardly believe it. All I was taking were barbs. I felt as if I'd been nearly dead for about six weeks and I'd come back to life. I was still a bit tired, but that was nothing. I was coping without smack. Or was I?

So I was off heroin. I wasn't a junkie any more. I was free. But free for what? What was life all about? What was the point in being free? Who cared whether I was stoned out of my brain or not? A great gaping emptiness had opened up inside me. It was painful. Intolerably painful.

There was a growing gnawing at my mind and body. An obsessive craving. I knew of only one thing that could cure it . . . smack.

Before long I was thinking about smack night and day. I was over my hepatitis now. I'd been here two whole months. I'd certainly had my rest—nearly didn't get up again. No, I had to have heroin. It was the only way to peace for me.

Roger had finally made his way back home and was thrilled at the changes in me. He couldn't see my mental torment.

'Jode, you're crazy to go back,' he pleaded. 'Stay here and get your act together while you can.'

'No, I'm going.' I replied.

Roger doesn't understand. He thinks it's only dope that's the hassle. The biggest problem really is this agonising emptiness inside me. It's been there ever since Jono died. The only time it goes away is when I'm stoned on smack. That's why I love it so much. I hate it because it's killing me. But I love it because it's the only happiness I've experienced since Jonothan's death. Nothing else can ever make me happy again.

So, with slightly shaky hands, I packed up and headed for the airport.

Chapter Eight

The plane swooped through the clouds high over Sydney. The lights below us twinkled in all directions radiating out from the dark tentacled centre which was the Harbour.

'Isn't it magnificent!' the woman next to me breathed excitedly.

I sighed. It didn't look magnificent to me, but dark and menacing. A hard, cruel city. But it had become my home, and the streets of the Cross were my 'workplace'. There, within hours, I'd be able to get the money I needed again for a fix.

I climbed wearily off the plane. My body felt heavy. The hepatitis had left me wrecked, and it was still in my bloodstream. 'Your liver's a mess,' the doctor had said, giving me a knowing look.

And it felt like it too. But it was time to get back to work. I was longing for the blissful escape of smack again.

The flat was dark and felt strangely empty when I arrived. 'Roxanne?' I called. No answer. A nameless wave of panic hit me, almost tangibly. 'Roxy, where are you?' Roxanne must be out, I thought. Probably working.

Oh Roxy, couldn't you be here when I came home? It feels so empty here without you. I hate it. The walls are closing in on me. It's dark. Oh God, I'll have to get out and get some money. I need a fix.

I tidied my hair and changed into something more eye-catching. Within minutes I was out on the street waiting for my first client again. I'd lost count of how many clients I needed now just to get that money to 'score'. But after several hours I had the money and was on Tom's doorstep. He grinned—an ugly, unfriendly grin—when he saw me.

'Well, the New Zealand chick's back again. Welcome home, sweetheart. We've missed you. We need you on the streets.'

By that time I was hanging out too much to care what he said.

I didn't even feel the needle in my arm or the sudden churn in my stomach. All I felt was relief as all my anger, and Mum, and New Zealand, and my revulsion towards men, retreated to a comfortable distance. My mind and my whole being were cushioned safely against reality again.

I believed I would die from heroin some day, like Kelly and Shana. But what was the alternative? None.

Several days passed, and still no sign of Roxanne. I was beginning to worry. Surely she wouldn't work, even on a ship, for so long?

Every time I heard the filthy floorboards in the hallway creak, I'd jump up ready to greet her. Several times I even poked my head out into the dark passageway, hoping she might be coming. Once Big Bob was walking towards me, instead.

He laughed in his coarse, mocking laugh. 'Hoping to get a few extras at his hour, Sexy? You must be desperate.'

I slammed the door in his face without bothering to answer. At the sharp sound, a mouse scurried across the floor from the cupboard to the bathroom. I shuddered and poured a glass of claret. The filth, when I was clear-headed enough even to see it, was beginning to revolt me. A high-pitched hollow laugh from the girls in the next flat echoed through the emptiness of the dark rooms. I sighed. How long till Roxy's warmth, what was left of it, and her buoyant, matter-of-fact nature made this hole home again?

The days passed. And the weeks.

Roxanne never came back. She was never heard of again.

Probably at the bottom of the Harbour. Some bastard sailor probably beat her up and chucked her overboard. Oh God. Poor Roxy. She was my only real friend. I can't bear it without her. I can't handle this scene by myself. Maybe I'll be dead soon, too.

I went over to Chris and Liz's flat. It was a cold, windy afternoon and the whole building felt like a refrigerator. It took all my energy to climb the stairs to their dark, damp little third floor flat. They were sitting on the floor in the lounge, stoned on heroin.

'Chris!' The fear in my voice made me sound abrupt. 'Have you seen Roxanne?'

She frowned at me. 'Not lately. Why?'

'She's gone.' The words sounded as hollow as I felt.

'What do you mean "gone"?'

'She hasn't been home since I came back from New Zealand. I'm scared. She must have OD'd. Or been beaten up and chucked in the Harbour. I always hated her working on those ships.'

Chris shrugged. She was too far out of it on dope to share my concern. 'I haven't seen her,' she repeated.

Liz was a bit more together. She looked at me sympathetically. 'Here, have some smack, Jodie. It'll help. I earned a bit extra last night. You can pay me back another time.'

I looked at her suspiciously. What did she want? Nobody trusted anybody else in this scene. I wasn't hanging out for a fix, and I had some dope at home. 'No thanks,' I said quietly. 'I'll be okay.'

I returned to my dingy flat. As I prepared my fix, I looked at my arms in disgust. The veins had almost disappeared. I clenched and unclenched my fist and found a good vein in my hand. Soon I was floating again.

One afternoon my sleep was interrupted by a sharp rap at the door. I stumbled out and looked through the peephole. It was the police. Maybe, just maybe, they knew something about Roxy. I'd chance it. I opened the door.

'Jodie Cadman?' It was more a statement than a question. I didn't answer.

'You're under arrest.'

'What for?'

'Using heroin.' They dragged me roughly away. I swore at them in fury, as they pushed me into a prison cell.

The night in prison was long. Long and sleepless. I was too accustomed to working at night and sleeping in the day. I felt exhausted, though; too tired even to care that I was in prison. My emotions were numb. I'd had about as much as I could take.

The next morning Tom was there, his hair combed for the first time in weeks probably, to bail me out. I had no illusions about his motives.

It was torture back on the streets without Roxy. I felt more alone than ever, even though I moved in with Chris and Liz. I hated the guys who came to me. My revulsion was increasing, and one night I ran from the room, sick, with a client there. He grabbed me later and beat me up till I was bruised and bleeding.

I was bashed up by several guys during the next few weeks. Most nights now I was terrified. So many of my clients were real weirdos.

Jim asked me to let Dave, a friend of his, stay for a few nights. 'He's just passing through, Jodie, and he just needs a bed for a night or two.'

After he left, I reached for my wallet to buy a hamburger. It was empty. Hundreds and hundreds of dollars. I'd worked my guts out for nights for that money and this guy had just cleaned me right out. Panic and desolation swept over me. It was all the money I had to score.

God, the whole world's falling apart around me. My life's just disintegrating. Roxy gone. Being beaten up. Ripped off. All these kinks and freaks to cope with. And I still feel sick all the time. The bottom's fallen out. I don't know where to turn. Everyone seems to be against me. Got to get the money to score though. I'll have to earn some fast, or I'll be hanging out.

The next day I was so depressed I couldn't bear it. 'Maybe a day out somewhere would help,' I thought. 'I can't stand this filthy hole.' So I caught a bus to Watsons Bay. The trip was pleasant, but I was numb inside. My eyes looked at the brilliant blue of the sun-sparkling Harbour, but I felt nothing. Not a thing. I might as well have been dead. A man sat next to me and moved over close to me so his leg was touching mine. Violent anger welled up inside me.

I'll kill you if you move any closer, you scum. Animal. I hate you. I hate all men. You touch me and I'll kill you. Kill you, kill you, kill you. Oh God, what am I turning into? A murderer now? God, I can't stand it. I hate him. People are just animals. Specially men. But what does that make me?

I wandered around aimlessly at Watsons Bay, trying to absorb the beauty. But nothing seemed to penetrate the hard shell that shut me in. The emptiness inside me was agonising. I walked out on a jetty and looked down at the water, slowly swirling, oily and dark green beneath me.

Just one step and I could be in the Harbour. I wouldn't even try to swim. I'd just sink. The dark, silent waters would swallow me. Nobody would ever know. Just like Roxanne. Oh God, where's Roxy now?

But the thought of death still terrified me, and I walked away and caught the bus home.

I was often in pain still as my abdomen had

suffered so badly from 'work'. I had V.D., and still the tired, nauseated remains of hepatitis.

Memories of Jonothan and Roxanne tormented me. I'd just be drifting off to sleep and I'd hear Jonothan's voice talking to me. 'Jodie, Why? Why heroin? Jodie, how can you sell yourself? You were class, Sis. You're killing yourself,' his voice would say. It would echo around and around in my mind, till I was hysterical.

I had visions of Roxy floating in the Harbour. Roxy, dead now like Jonothan.

Why did you die and leave me, Roxy? How could you leave me alone in this pit? I want to die, but I'm scared. Scared of what's on the other side. Will I see you again if I die, Roxy? Jonothan? What if there's a hell? But this is hell already. It couldn't be worse. Oh God, I can't take any more. I can't, I can't, I can't.

I'd given up the idea of finding a guy to support me. In fact, I'd totally given up on men. Even on women. I didn't want or trust anyone. It was just me against the world. All I wanted was dope.

I decided to overdose properly. I took heroin, then frantically grabbed all the pills I could find—serepax, downers, everything. I jumped into the car and went out driving. Anywhere. Just driving. The lights of the Cross swirled past me at a dizzy rate. Then everything went swimming and I fell asleep and crashed into another car.

Through the nauseating waves of darkness, I could hear muffled shouting. Someone was angry. Then rough hands dragged me from the car, dumped me on the footpath and left me there.

Slowly I struggled to my feet in a haze of drugs and shock. There was a house in darkness right beside me. I staggered across the yard, too dazed to find an open window, and punched my hand straight through the glass of a side window and opened it. Clumsily I climbed in. My body felt like a dead weight as I hauled myself over the window sill. I headed for the phone and rang my current flatmates.

Chris answered. 'What do you want?'

'Look, man, I don't know where the hell I am,' I said. 'I've OD'd, but I don't really want to die.'

'Typical,' said Chris and slammed the phone down in my ear.

A sinking terror gripped me at the thought of that endless (or was it?) dark abyss called death.

I grabbed some jewellery and a radio and some clothes—it was almost an automatic reaction now. Then I stumbled out onto the road and hailed a taxi and got home.

Chris and Liz took one look at me. Blood dripping everywhere from cutting my hand on the window pane; jewellery, radio and clothing clutched in my arms; and me swaying like a drunkard.

'Get that hot stuff out of this place,' Chris whispered fiercely. 'We don't want you. You can get out too.'

She and Liz started throwing my things out the door.

'Man you can't be serious,' I choked out. 'Here am I, I've just OD'd, and you're kicking me out.'

Liz looked at me wearily. 'Yeah, we've had a gutful of you,' she said.

So that was it. I had nowhere to go. Suddenly the waves of dizziness overwhelmed me and everything went black. I collapsed on the floor.

I was in a long dark tunnel ... sinking ... sinking. Somewhere, from a long way away, I heard voices. Harsh, frightened voices. 'She's going to die, the bitch. We've got to get her out of here.'

'What'll we do with her?'

'Take her to a hospital.'

They dragged me into a car and took me to a hospital and dumped me there. They hurried away. I wasn't conscious enough to work out where I was. There were more voices somewhere out there. Then darkness engulfed me and the voices disappeared as I sank into oblivion.

Chapter Nine

Waves of darkness were sweeping over me with a giddy, nauseating insistence. Sometimes the darkness parted and harsh white light glared at me. Then I would sink back into the welcome embrace of darkness again.

Then it was daylight, but everything blurred in and out of focus. Someone was bending over me. Muffled voices were talking. Gradually the blurred forms came into focus. They were women in white uniforms. And a man, also in white. The horrible reality of my situation became clear. I really was in hospital.

Oh God, why didn't you let me die? All I wanted was to die. Hospital, of all places! I might as well be in bloody prison. I'm so tired. I just want to sleep. Maybe I still am going to die.

But, day by day, I became clearer in my mind and I knew I was not going to die. Not yet, anyway. I was still trapped in that hideous torment of not wanting to live, but being too scared to die.

The hospital treated me for V.D. and hepatitis, once the overdose had worn off. They were giving me pethidine regularly to blot out my abdominal pain—and unknowingly helping to support my heroin addiction. Most of the nurses were cool, efficient and a bit aloof. Obviously they regarded me as something less than human. I watched them scurrying briskly around in their uniforms. They might have been creatures from another planet.

I was intolerably lonely. There was not one friend to come and visit me. One day Janie, one of the slightly more friendly nurses, walked in cheerily. 'Visitor for you, Jodie,' she said. My heart quickened. A visitor. Who knew I was there? Who cared?

It was Tom. One look at his steely eyes told me he wasn't there to comfort me. He waited till Janie was out of earshot.

'What the hell do you think you're doing Jodie? Having a little rest, eh? Well hurry up and get out of this place. We need you on the streets.'

He looked at me menacingly. I blinked at his

cruel face and knew he was capable of anything. Anything as long as the money for smack kept coming in. He threw me a small bag of dope. 'Here,' he grinned cruelly. 'You'll be needing this. You'll get more when you get out.'

I turned away and looked out the window as he walked out. Tears ran helplessly down my face. I was so lonely. Nobody cared. Not a soul. Sobs welled up convulsively.

I looked at the window. Janie had told me I was on the tenth floor. Maybe I would jump from the window. I swung my skinny legs over the side of the bed and stood up shakily. Slowly I groped my way over to the window and looked out. Out and down. I looked giddily at the ant-like people swarming about in the streets far below. If I could just haul myself up onto that window sill. Would I have the courage to jump? What would happen to me? Would I die of fright as I plummeted through the air? Would I be just a body that splattered onto the footpath below? Would the real me be still alive somewhere? Where?

Was there another life on the other side of death? Maybe even heaven and hell like some religious people thought. What about God? Was he real? I'd always had a nebulous sort of awareness of God, without ever being able to work out if he was real, or who he was if he was real. I'd always figured he must be punishing me, if he existed, by putting me into this torture called life. If he was real, why didn't he do something about all my suffering? And all the other people's suffering?

> *Jonothan lying on the hospital bed. Roxy floating in the Harbour. Shana. Kelly. God, I can't take any more. I want to die. But I'm still scared of what's on the other side. Oh God, I'm terrified. I don't want to live and I'm too scared to die. God, if you're out there, help me. If you're really real, **help** me!*

Somehow, as my mind had wandered over my desperate situation, something strange had crystallised inside me. As my whole insides reached out in a cry for help, I almost knew that this time I was talking to somebody real—somebody who was listening. Or I certainly hoped so. God was my last chance. There was no other way out.

I walked slowly back to my bed. Suddenly I started tingling all over. At first I was almost frightened. It was an unfamiliar sensation to my tired, abused body. As the tingling went on, sobs began to well up from the very pit of my being. Tears streamed down my face and I sobbed uncontrollably for two whole days.

Memories began to flood my mind. I felt like a drowning person, reliving my whole life as I cried and cried. There was Jonothan, riding past in the brilliant sun. Jonothan lying white, lifeless, on a hospital bed. Jonothan's bike a mangled heap of metal.

'I never wanted a girl. I can't bear to touch Jodie.' Oh Mum, why didn't you want me? Why couldn't you love me? Why did you push me away when I came to hug you?

There was Roxanne, laughing. 'Try prostitution, Jode, it's good money. What've you got to lose?' Roxanne, clinging to me for comfort after a long night's work. Tom, grinning maliciously. Big Bob, laughing his ugly laugh. Guys leering. Guys angry. Guys I'd ripped off. Guys who'd ripped me off. Guys . . .

After two days of reliving literally hundreds of experiences and relationships, my mind started to focus on one thing. It was a name. A name that impressed itself indelibly on my consciousness and refused to budge. It was John, my cousin in Brisbane. The Christian—a 'religious freak' I'd always laughed at and avoided. I tried to ignore the name, but it would not go away. At last I decided to ring him. Perhaps I could go and stay with him for a break, get my life together, then come back here and start all over again. I found the phone in the hospital corridor. It was about 8 pm as I dialled his number. His voice sounded strangely warm and friendly.

I thought quickly. I certainly couldn't tell him the truth. Well, I was a skilful liar now. 'John,' I said shakily into the phone, 'I'm in hospital. I was beaten up. Do you think I could come and stay with you for a while to recover?' I told him where I was and hung up, and wandered back to my room expecting to get a message back from him or to see him in a few days. I slipped into the first peaceful sleep I'd had in weeks.

The next morning, soon after the breakfast trolley was wheeled away, John appeared in my room. 'What on earth are you doing here so quickly?' I asked, taken off guard.

John hesitated. 'I was in the middle of a prayer meeting when you rang, Jodie. We prayed for you and God impressed on us that you were in trouble and that I should come straight down and get you.'

For once I was stuck for words. I just stared at him.

'It's all right. I *know* what you've been doing, Jodie,' he said. 'God gave me a fair idea of where you're at. I want to help you.'

I freaked and blurted out the truth. '*You* want to help *me*? Man, I sell myself on the streets at night to get money. I stick needles in my arm for a hobby. I've got V.D. I'm filth.'

John didn't bat an eyelid. He just looked at me and said, 'Jodie, I love you and I want to help you. I'm going to take you back with me.'

It was too much. I began to cry again. 'Anyway,' I sobbed, 'you can't take me to Queensland because I'm out on bail.'

This unbelievable guy was still undeterred. 'It's okay, I'll go and see the police. I'm sure they'll give me permission to take you.'

And they did. That was a miracle in itself. I was beginning to think that perhaps God was real and that he was responsible for all the strange things that had happened during the past few days.

Before long, I was at John's place in Brisbane. But the haven of a peaceful Christian home was not yet for me. John was keen for me to repent and become a Christian. I was not ready for this, but I said the right words just to keep him happy. I had begun, too, to withdraw from all the drugs, and my mind was going crazy.

After a day or so, I could stand it no longer. I was starting to think John was the devil and he was out to get me. So I left him. I took refuge in a Salvation Army Women's Hostel, and started to plan my return to the streets to get money for a fix.

The next morning I went out latish. Tired.

I sat at a bus-stop in the Valley. I would have to make some money fast. I was hanging out badly. The streets of the Valley looked like a good place to get clients. I sighed and looked down at my long red-painted fingernails, tight jeans, low-cut black blouse. Yes, I looked okay.

Have I come all that way just to go back to this? Was that really God doing all those things in hospital? Where's that creep John at? Is he a Moonie or something? Maybe Christians are just like Moonies or some other cult. More fool me for getting my hopes up. John was always nagging me about some place called Teen Challenge. Probably just another cult. How would you know whether to trust them? I'll make some money here and go back to the Cross. It's the only place I know, now. It's hell, but it's home.

A voice interrupted my thoughts. An elderly couple were gazing at me with concerned faces. 'Are you all right, dear?' the woman asked. 'We couldn't help noticing you seem upset or something.'

I opened my mouth to say I was fine and found myself blurting out, 'No, I'm not okay. I'm a heroin addict and I need a fix. I don't really know this place. I work in Kings Cross.'

By this time tears had started running down my face and the couple seemed genuinely to care. They didn't even look shocked. I kept talking, and ended out telling them practically my whole life story.

'I don't suppose you know the way to Teen Challenge?' I asked apprehensively.

They did! Was it a coincidence?

'It's in Paddington, dear. Just get a Bardon bus and get off in the main shopping centre. Cross over the road and it's in the little arcade there. You can't miss it.'

'Have you got money for your bus fare?' the man asked.

'No,' I gulped.

They gave me the money. Soon a Bardon bus roared into the stop. I waved to them as I jolted away towards Paddington and Teen Challenge.

I sat with clenched fists as more and more people boarded the bus. How far was Paddington? I'd asked the driver to tell me when we were there. We lurched and swayed around a winding road. It seemed interminable, but it wasn't really far at all. I began to panic.

What have I done? Where's Paddington? The other end of the earth, probably. Could be any God-forsaken dump. I wonder if it's like Paddo in Sydney. The trendy place full of arty people. Plenty of dope around there, too. What if Teen Challenge is real? What if they're all telling the truth and they can help me? How would I know? Oh God, if you're really real and Teen Challenge is okay and Christians are real and not Moonies or cults or anything, I want you to let me know. Get them to ask me to stay with them straight away. Tonight!'

'Paddington!' shouted the busdriver.
Suddenly I was terrified. I groped my way to the front of the bus on shaking legs and climbed down. The bus roared away and I crossed the busy road. Sure enough, just as they'd said, there was a little arcade. I could see a sign, *Teen Challenge*, halfway down, on the left.
I paused outside. Certainly nothing flash about the place. Just like a little shop in an arcade. Oh well, what the heck? What would I tell them? I must have been crazy to have come here, I thought. What was I letting myself in for?

But I'd come too far to turn back. I took a deep breath, pushed open the door, and hurried inside. A friendly-looking girl sat at the desk, sorting papers.

'I want to see the person in charge,' I blurted out. 'Right now. It's urgent.'

'Charles!' she called. 'There's a girl here who says she needs to see you urgently.'

'Oh. Okay. Show her in,' said a quiet male voice.

I followed the girl into a pleasant dimly-lit room. In the corner sat a dark-haired, bearded man with large, solemn eyes. He motioned for me to sit down on one of the comfortable chairs.

'I'm Charles Ringma,' he said with the hint of a twinkle in those solemn eyes.

I didn't know where to start. I just stared at him and then out it all came. 'You've got to help me,' I said. 'I'm hooked on heroin and I'm hanging out for a fix. My whole insides are tied in a knot. I'm going crazy.'

The man, who hadn't taken his eyes off me, didn't appear shocked or even surprised. 'Where do you live?' he asked.

'Kings Cross. But I can't handle it any longer. It's the only home I know though. Everything's fallen apart. I've been beaten up, ripped off, my best friend's dead. I've got V.D. and hepatitis . . .'

The words were tumbling out so fast I hardly knew what I was saying. But Charles gave the occasional nod or raised his eyebrows, so I gathered he probably understood.

'I don't know where to go or what to do,' I continued. 'I don't know who I can trust. I don't even know who I am any longer.' By now I was sobbing as I talked.

Charles seemed amazingly unruffled by my outburst. Didn't he even care?

'How do I even know I can trust you?' I shouted at him. 'You're just sitting there. How do I know where you're at?'

'You don't know yet,' he replied calmly. 'You'll have to give us all time to show you where we're at, won't you.'

'I haven't *got* any time,' I yelled. 'I'm hanging out for a fix. I'm desperate. I need help *now*.'

'You'll get it,' he replied. He paused briefly and asked, 'Would you like a cup of tea or coffee?'

'Coffee, please.'

Does this guy realise how serious this is? Does he know I'm for real? He's sitting there as cool as you like. Oh well, I've told him everything now.

Charles went out and came back with two cups of coffee. 'Well, you need a rest for a start,' he said, as I sipped the welcome warm brew. 'How about staying with a few of the girls from Teen Challenge tonight, and I'll come and see you tomorrow and we'll take it from there.'

I was blown out. Had I heard right? Was God

real? And was he really making all these things happen? Maybe he really would help me to have a happy life. And maybe Christianity was 'the real thing' and not just some cult.

A strange mixture of relief, desperation and apprehension overwhelmed me as we drove to the girls' flat. I was really hanging out for a fix, but I decided to trust this guy. For as long as I could handle it, anyway.

Charles introduced me to two friendly girls and left me there with them. They served me a delicious-looking meal, but I was feeling too sick to eat much. Robyn and Debbie seemed so pleasant, I wasn't sure whether to trust them or not. What if I was being sucked into a cult? Would they accept me, even if they were the real thing? Would I be able to handle them any better than I'd handled John? Anyway, I could always split and go back to Sydney.

Debbie showed me into a small, attractively furnished bedroom. 'Looks like an early night would do you good,' she smiled.

'See you in the morning.'

I crawled into the narrow but comfortable bed, exhausted after my emotion-packed day.

God, have I gone mad? What am I doing here? Who am I? Who are you, God? Was that really you answering my prayers? Well, I guess they were prayers. It couldn't all just be coincidence. The past week has just blown me out, God. Man, I'm going into withdrawal. I feel so sick. What's going to happen to me?'

In the early hours of the morning I fell into an exhausted sleep, wondering what the next day would bring.

Chapter Ten

I groaned and rolled over. Harsh sunlight was streaming through the open window onto my face. My head was aching. I was wet with perspiration. Even the sheets felt damp. I buried my face in the pillow to escape the assault on my eyeballs.

Where was I? That's right. Staying with some girls from Teen Challenge. Whatever Teen Challenge really was. John had said something about drug rehabilitation centres. I shuddered. My body and mind were withdrawing from the pethidine and other drugs which had replaced smack during my week in hospital. Waves of nausea swept over me.

From somewhere in the flat I could hear someone singing. A girl's voice. Sounded okay. But all sounds were grating on my nerves now.

There was a knock at the bedroom door. I was tempted to roll over and ignore it, but I sighed and called, 'Come in,' in a voice that sounded strangely shaky and hollow.

Debbie came in carrying a tray with some toast and a cup of tea on it. I looked at it, so prettily set out, with a little bunch of flowers on the tray, and wondered if I could swallow the toast and keep it down.

'It's ten o'clock,' said Debbie cheerfully. 'I let you sleep in because I know you're not feeling well, but Charles rang and he's coming to see you at eleven. Have something to eat, and then you might feel like getting showered and dressed.'

'Charles . . .?' I asked vaguely. 'Oh, the guy who brought me here. That's right, he said he'd come and see me. I'd forgotten. My mind's going around in circles. Okay, thanks. I'll get up in a minute.'

Is that voice me talking? The words are still hanging in the air as if they came from nowhere. It doesn't even sound like my voice. God, I'm frightened. Feel like I'm going out of my mind. Feel like I don't even exist any more. There's no 'me', only this crazy prison of confusion and pain. Maybe this is what

Casey felt like when they chucked her in the loony bin.'

With shaky hands, I picked up a piece of toast and nibbled at it, and sipped the hot tea. Debbie came back in with a cup of tea and sat on a chair near the bed.

'Man, I don't know if I'm hot or cold,' I said. 'I'm dripping with perspiration but I feel really weird.'

Debbie nodded sympathetically. 'It's going to be a hot day,' she said. 'Are you used to Queensland summers?'

I shook my head.

'Well, they're hot. You've probably missed the worst of it. It was stinking hot in February.'

I nodded vaguely, watching this friendly, pretty girl with short dark hair and wondering where she was really coming from.

Soon I was showered and dressed back into my jeans and blouse. Charles arrived and Debbie showed us both into the lounge and left us alone.

'So, how're you feeling?' Charles asked.

'Awful,' I groaned. 'How the hell do you think I feel? Man, I'm withdrawing from all that dope and my head's going crazy. I don't even know who I am. I hardly even know whether I'm really here or not. And I don't know who to trust any more. I don't know who's from God and who's from the devil and who's a cult or who's a Christian, and who's my friend or my enemy. I'm going to go mental.'

Charles listened quietly and then said, 'You're going to be okay. You'll just have to hang in there till you're through the worst of the withdrawal. I can't make you trust us. That's something you'll have to decide for yourself. But if I were in your shoes I'd give it a go.'

I stared at him hopelessly. Didn't he have any real answers? Was this all the help Christians had to offer? Was I crazy to trust him?

'I'd like you to have a short rest in hospital before we settle you anywhere else,' he continued.

'Hospital!' I yelled. 'Man, I've just come from hospital. God got me out of hospital and now you want to chuck me back in again. You've got to be joking.'

Charles fingered his beard, then continued calmly, 'It won't be like the hospital in Sydney. We'll come and visit you every day and one of the Teen Challenge psychiatrists may be able to help you sort out a few things while you're in there. You need medical attention, anyway, don't you? You told me yourself you're getting over hepatitis and you've got V.D., not to mention the drug withdrawal. I know it's not an easy step for you, Jodie, but you won't regret it.'

So, it was hospital or split and go back to the Cross. Some choice. I was hanging out so badly I'd have to get money to score before I went anywhere. Oh well, I'd come this far, so I might as well risk it and do what this guy wanted.

'Okay,' I muttered.

Charles took me to a Brisbane hospital and I was admitted to the psychiatric ward. I took one look at the 'fruitcakes' and kinky people in there and freaked right out. But it was too late. I was signed into the hospital. And I was feeling sick. Really sick. I watched Charles walk away and thought, 'I suppose that's the last I'll see of him. He's just dumped me here.'

It was like a nightmare at first. I kept hearing voices inside my head—loud, tormenting voices; confusing voices. Fear gripped my insides and I kept expecting someone to jump up from behind me and attack me.

That bloody weirdo's ugly face at my bedroom window. Leering at me. Footsteps echoing in the dark hall outside the flat. Me plunging the carving knife at the face at the window. Plunging, plunging, hysterically. People following me. Kinky guys beating me ...

I was wary of the other patients. 'If any of those fruitcakes come near me, I'll kill them,' I told the nurses. But nobody came near me.

Charles' friend, the psychiatrist, kept his eye on me and he seemed okay. He was easy to talk to.

Charles came up to see me nearly every day during my ten days in hospital. When he couldn't come, someone else from Teen Challenge would come.

I wasn't too keen on the idea of those other

visitors initially. My first visitor apart from Charles was a lady called Sue Paulsen. A brown-haired lady, several years older than I was, who sat and chattered happily to me, smiling with big blue twinkling eyes. I just stared back at her. Who did she think she was to come in here and ask me how I was? She could see for herself how I was. Did she expect me to spill my guts to her and tell her all about my life in the Cross? Maybe they all thought I was free entertainment. Some sort of circus performer or something.

Then Margie came. I was sitting on a chair near the window, looking out over the depressing rows of houses and busy streets, when a nurse called out, 'Visitor, Jodie.' Suddenly I felt very small and frightened. I braced myself and turned around.

'Hi, Jodie, I'm Margie. Margie Robertson,' said a bright, warm voice. I stared at her. Just a normal looking chick—long, straight, dark hair and a few freckles; friendly brown eyes; jeans and a floral blouse. Was she part of Teen Challenge too? I felt aware, for the first time, of my low-cut black blouse and my long red fingernails. How much did this girl know about me? Would any normal people want to know someone who worked the streets?

She pulled up a chair near mine. 'I'm from *Koinonia*,' she said.

'Koinonia? Oh, that's that place where that other woman, Sue, lives,' I replied dully. 'A drug rehabilitation centre.' There was a scathing note in my voice, but Margie ignored it.

'Yes. Susie and her husband, Neil, run Koinonia at the moment. I live there. I'm on the staff. It's a great place.'

I looked at her distrustfully. What did 'on the staff' entail, I wondered. What did these people want from me?

'How are you finding it here in the hospital?' Margie asked.

I opened my mouth to rebuff her with some glib reply, but her brown eyes looked so earnest I found myself telling her the truth.

Margie was a sympathetic listener. She really seemed to understand. Stranger still, she seemed to accept me. I didn't feel she was judging me and, like Charles, she seemed totally unrattled as, little by little, I told her my story. Unlike Charles, she was quite open in showing her feelings. Although nothing I said shocked her, she often had tears in her eyes as we talked.

It was a new experience for me, talking openly about my life and my feelings and sensing that someone really cared about what I was saying— and about me. I was actually disappointed when it was time for her to leave, although I bluffed my way through it so she wouldn't know.

'I'll come back in a few days,' she called gaily as she left.

'If you like,' I said.

Charles kept coming, too, much to my amazement. He really seemed to care. The psychiatrist, also a Christian, talked to me often. I was blown out. These two guys were my friends. They wanted what was best for me. They weren't making any money out of me. It was unreal.

Sometimes after talking to Charles or Margie or the psychiatrist, I had the oddest feeling. It was as if sunshine was creeping inside me with its warmth and light. I was almost happy. But I was still tormented by memories. And nightmares. And voices in my head. I dreaded the darkness as it approached each evening.

Jonothan's dead. Nothing's ever been the same since Jono died. Nobody will ever replace him. Why did he have to die? What's life all about? What's the point in it all? Roxy floating in the Harbour. Robbie's eyes, old and resigned. Robbie behind bars. Me behind bars. Real bars, with Mum on the other side. The bars are just as real now, but nobody can see them. Will I ever get out of this cage?

'You're pretty aggressive towards the other patients,' the psychiatrist commented. 'Are you scared of them?'

'Man, I'm not crazy, you know,' I told him. 'I might be a bit crazy at the moment, but I'm not that crazy. If any of those fruitcakes come near me, I'll smash their heads in.'

So he continued to ensure that none of them did come near me. I found myself living for his and Charles' visits. It was so incredible being able to be totally honest with these guys and to trust them. Just as long as they weren't going to start ramming religion down my throat.

'I don't want to talk about Jesus,' I told them both. 'I'm nearly out of my brain as it is, without trying to make sense of all that religious garbage.'

It was funny how I'd come to accept God but not Jesus. I was pretty sure God was real and he was sort of looking after me. Strange, after all those years of running away from him and doing everything which I knew was probably wrong. Yet, underneath it all, I think I'd always hoped he was there somewhere. But then I'd be torn apart again by the never ending question. If he was real, why had he put me in this hell of a life? What had I done to deserve it? It was too much for me even to try to work out, so I'd always turned away from thinking about him.

Now here I was, more or less believing in him. But I wasn't at all sure about Jesus. Who was to say he was any different from any of the other good guys—or weirdos—who'd started cults? And the idea of being caught in a cult really freaked me.

So the psychiatrist and Charles respected where I was at. They talked about Teen Challenge instead. About the addicts who had been helped and were living straight lives now. About this Koinonia place. Sounded like a real mansion. They seemed convinced that Teen Challenge could help me and that I'd like it there.

'I don't know.' I was hesitant. Confused. 'Sydney's the only place I really know. I don't want to go back to that hell hole, but it's all I know, now.'

'So you don't really want to stay off heroin at all?' Charles asked. 'Is that what you're saying?'

'I do and I don't. It's the only way of life I know. Man, if I stay straight and don't go back onto the streets, I won't know who I am. I'll be like a little baby having to learn to live all over again.'

'Yes, I realise that. But you'd have caring people helping you to learn,' Charles replied. He looked at me with a half smile. 'I think you'd be surprised at how quickly you'd learn, too. But you'll have to decide whether you really want to get off the stuff for good, or not. Otherwise we're wasting our time.'

'Nobody said you had to come in here every day and see me!' I retorted.

'I said *our* time,' Charles replied patiently. 'Yours, too. It's your life, Jodie. But the decisions you make now will probably affect the rest of your life. What do you actually want out of life?'

I sighed and fought back tears. What did I want out of life? 'I guess I really would like to be able to live without dope,' I said. 'I keep imagining myself as a little child with a mother on one side and a father on the other. I'm holding their hands. That's what I'd really like. To be part of a happy family. To have the security and love I never had when I was a kid.'

'Well, that probably would come through other relationships,' Charles replied. 'The first step towards knowing security and love is to stop wiping yourself out with dope. There's a lot more to life than you've experienced. You can be happy and fulfilled without drugs. Think about it seriously. You've only got a few more days left in here. I'll be back tomorrow.'

God, he hardly ever mentions you. I guess that's because I screamed at him about not talking religion. Was it you who got me here, God? And led me to these people? I'm still scared of walking into something so totally different from anything I've known. But you must have a purpose for my life, God. Otherwise you could've let me die in Sydney. Help me to make the right decision. I don't want to go to that Koinonia place and then find I can't handle it and I've got nowhere to go.

Waves of peace swept over me and my eyes filled with tears. I cried every time I thought and wondered about God; and I found myself thinking about him often, now.

Then I would try to weigh up the advantages of returning to Sydney or not. Some days I'd remember the good things—the Harbour sparkling on a sunny day; early days when Roxy and I were close friends and we'd sit and talk and sip red wine. But more often I'd remember all those demented guys and the terror of being followed, so many of my friends dying, and the unbearable loneliness.

*What **have** I got? Charles is right. I haven't really got much. Nothing worthwhile. What's the point of life? What is life?*

While Charles was busily encouraging me to live in this Koinonia—this place that sounded like heaven, a beautiful big old house on the riverbank—the psychiatrist faithfully made me face up to where I was at and stop deluding myself.

'How do you really feel about those guys?' he'd ask. 'You're angry with them, aren't you?'

Reluctantly, I admitted I was. Angry with the guys who'd been my clients, angry with Tom and all the drug dealers, angry with my mother. Just plain angry.

'So what!' I said. 'I've been angry all my life. There's nothing I can do about it.'

'Yes, there is,' the psychiatrist insisted gently. 'You don't have to live with all that anger. If you let Teen Challenge really help you, you can get free of it.'

So, with this growing hope of changing all the attitudes and feelings that plagued me, and spurred on by Charles' depicting this heaven-on-earth place which awakened an incredible longing in me as well as stirring my curiosity, I began to change.

Before Charles was due to arrive on my

second last day in hospital, Margie came again. Much to my embarrassment, I found myself fighting tears. She didn't have to come. She didn't even know me. But she seemed genuinely glad to see me. For some reason, I trusted her.

'I hope you decide to come to live with us,' she said earnestly. 'Honestly, Jodie, you'd love it. I know you would. There are beautiful big gardens. You could have a garden to grow flowers in, if you want.'

There it was again, this image of heaven.

'What about the other people there?' I asked. 'What are they like?'

Margie paused. She seemed to be looking for the right words. 'They're a really great bunch,' she said. 'A mixture of all different kinds of people.'

'Are they all dope freaks like me?'

'No. A few of them are. There's one guy just off heroin. He's from Sydney, too. Most of the others have had some sort of drug involvement, but maybe not to the same extent.'

'Well, what are they doing there if they haven't been junkies?' I asked.

'I suppose they all have, in one way or another, whether it's alcohol or pills or a bit of anything they can lay their hands on. They're all learning to live straight. To cope without depending on drugs.'

I bit back a scornful comment. We heroin users looked down on other drug users. Weaklings. But I realised I was in no position to say anything. Not at the moment anyway.

'I wouldn't know anyone. I wouldn't know who I could trust,' I said.

'Well, I'd be there!' said Margie with a laugh.

I thought for a minute. I enjoyed Margie's vibrant personality. It might be okay with her there. Doubts and conflicts assailed me.

'What's the point, though, really?' I asked. 'So I come and live at Koinonia with you guys. What's going to happen to me?'

'Jodie, you've seen for yourself how God's intervened in your life and rescued you out of the Sydney scene. He loves you, Jodie. He wants to change you so you can be a happy, together person without drugs.'

I was half cynical, half hopeful, but it seemed worth trying it. When Charles arrived, soon after Margie left, I was almost embarrassed. There was no point in trying to bluff my way with this guy. I always had the feeling that he could see what was really going on inside me.

'Well?' he asked.

'I'll give it a go,' I said.

'I'm really glad,' Charles answered. 'I'm sure you'll love it. And you'll be surprised how much it'll help you. I'll ring Neil and Sue and get them to pick you up tomorrow.

'Neil and Sue,' I thought. 'The bright, chatty lady ... and goodness knows how many other strangers.'

Charles talked for a few minutes and then left to see someone else. As he turned to walk away, my heart sank. Here he was, putting me in the hands of strangers—except Margie. How could I face them all?

Charles turned as he reached the doorway as if he had heard my thoughts. 'Don't worry, I'll stay in touch,' he said quietly. 'You'll be able to see me whenever you need to.'

Feeling reassured, I found myself looking forward to the next day. I'd be able to suss out this 'heaven on earth' for myself.

Chapter Eleven

*It's nine o'clock in the morning. A warm, balmy day in April, 1982. Time has stopped still for now as I stand here, waiting, between two different worlds. I'm twenty-three. And I feel like a little kid of about ten. Am I mad to go to Koinonia? I guess I'll soon find out. I can always split. Don't know where I'd go, though. These Teen Challenge people are my only real friends now. What if the other people at Koinonia can't handle me when they know about me? Charles says they're used to people like me. But will they **really** accept me? What if they freak out about my past? God, please make them like me.*

I grabbed my small packed bag and went to look out the window, waiting apprehensively for Neil and Sue to arrive. Margie came in with Sue. I was so relieved to see her now-familiar face, I almost burst into tears again.

'We're going on a picnic to Bribie', she announced. 'It's such a lovely day and it'll give you a chance to meet all the others you'll be living with. You know Sue, don't you?'

I nodded and smiled warily at Sue who smiled happily back.

They took me to a big, old, green van and put my bag in. I climbed in and was introduced to a motley-looking group of people. I decided to stay quiet for a while and check them out. No doubt they'd be checking me out, too. Bribie was okay. It was an island, but it was joined to the rest of the coast by a bridge that we drove over, so it didn't feel like an island. We had a picnic lunch on the beach. Everyone seemed to be enjoying themselves so much, it made me feel quite out of it. But after lunch some of them went for a swim, and Margie and I walked along the beach. A cool sea breeze whipped into our faces, and carried our voices away so we had almost to shout to each other. As usual, Margie was reassuring as I voiced my many doubts and fears.

Then we were back in the van going home. Home! Everyone called it 'home', just like a real home and a real family. At last I would see this little bit of heaven.

We wound around the tree-lined streets of Graceville. Finally we drove along a street on the riverbank and pulled in to a huge, old, white two-storeyed building. Sure enough there were beautiful gardens with trees and everything, sloping away in terraces down to the riverbank.

Soon we were eating dinner around a large old table. I was feeling on edge sitting with all these straight people, trying to act normally.

But then something really strange happened. Listening to all their conversations and answering the occasional question that came my way, suddenly I felt almost as if this really *was* my home, as if they wanted me there, and I belonged there.

Later that night Margie, with whom I shared a room, sat up late talking to me. I told her I was still hesitant about staying there.

'Oh, Jodie, stay,' she pleaded. 'We can really help you here. You've got to believe there's more to life than the sort of experiences you've had. If you do decide to go back to the Cross, what then? Where's it all leading? What does the future hold for you?'

I couldn't lie to her. 'Nothing,' I said, in a flat voice. 'There's nothing there for me really. It's just what I'm used to.'

She flung her arms around me. 'Well stay and get used to us here', she said. 'We really want you to.'

I was amazed again. This chick, who barely knew me, really cared. She had tears in her eyes.

I broke down and started crying, and couldn't stop until long after I was in bed and the lights were out.

I'd really like this place to be okay. As long as it's not a cult or anything crazy like that. I think I might like it here. Don't know how I'll cope without dope, though. What if they turn out to be freaks of some kind? I'll keep my bags half-packed in case I have to get away in a hurry.

The next day Neil and Sue took me aside. 'Well, what do you think?' asked Neil.

'I don't know,' I answered truthfully.

'Well, you can stay here for a week or so initially while you're making up your mind,' he continued. 'We'd like you to take part in all our activities and that includes church, devotions, household duties, the works. That way you'll get a realistic idea of what we're all about.'

'Okay,' I replied. 'But just don't talk religion to me. I'm not ready to handle that sort of stuff.'

'Don't worry,' Sue smiled, 'nobody's going to ram the Bible down your throat. We just want you to see how you like being one of us.'

So, with my bags half-packed in readiness for an escape, I settled in for a 'trial period'.

I enjoyed the sense of being at home there. The jobs they gave me during that first week weren't hard, as I guess they realised I still wasn't feeling all that well. Often in the afternoons I'd walk in the garden and collect bits of fern, flowers, pine cones, even pretty-looking twigs.

'Jodie, they're lovely,' exclaimed Sue as I walked in sheepishly with them for the first time. 'You can arrange some in the living room if you like.'

So I had fun arranging flowers and ferns. I'd never realised how beautiful all these simple little things were.

Most of that first week I stayed near Margie, day and night, often asking her the meaning of things people said. Even things about God. I trusted her. I still wasn't sure about the others. What if they were going to rip me off? Margie and I would talk till late most nights. She was interested in everything about me and my life, and told me various things about her own life.

By the end of the week I was convinced that I liked Koinonia. It was home. I enjoyed the sense of belonging. Besides, what did I have to return to in Sydney?

Having made this decision, I began to feel apprehensive. What if I blew it there and had nowhere to go? What if they ended out ripping me off? Or trying to turn me into some sort of religious freak?

It intrigued me that Neil and Sue wanted to run this place. They had three lovely daughters, the youngest still a tiny baby. Why would they want to live with all these other people? Weren't they scared for their daughters' safety with all these ex-dope freaks living there? But they didn't seem to be. In fact, they seemed remarkably happy.

Going to church on Sunday was a new experience. As I dressed for it the first time, I was shaking with nervousness. Man, what would church be like? What would all those straight people think of me?

We went to a church which had been started by Teen Challenge. 'Jubilee Fellowship', it was called. It was totally different from anything I expected. Most of the people dressed casually and everyone seemed relaxed and happy.

Then the singing started. I was taken off guard. Tears began to stream down my face as I sat amid enthusiastic singers belting out songs about Jesus. I kept seeing myself as a kid of twelve or thirteen. Vaguely I remembered attending a Christian camp with a school friend and making some sort of response to Jesus at the time. All the in-between years seemed to fall away and there I sat, just like that twelve-year-old Jodie, listening to the singing.

I cried all through church every week for the first month or so. Sometimes I didn't even know why I was crying, but I'd hear them talking about Jesus and tears would pour out of my eyes.

There was something about all the others at Koinonia that impresssed me. They were happy. Not hyped up, just happy. And they were at peace in themselves. They cared about one another. It really was like a family ... and I was a part of it, yet somehow not quite a part of it. Perhaps it was tied up with the religion bit.

Charles came out to visit us a week or so after I'd been there. 'So, how's it going?' he asked me.

'I don't know. Good, I suppose. I don't know if I'll ever really feel I'm "me" here, though. It's so different.'

Charles smiled. 'You mean different from walking around in a haze of drugs?'

'That's only part of it,' I replied. 'It's everything. The people. The things we do. Everything. I just don't know if it's real. For me, anyway.'

'Give it time, Jodie,' Charles replied gently. 'Give yourself a chance to adjust. You'll find you'll change, too, so you'll feel more a part of it.'

'That's one of the things I'm scared of,' I said. 'I'm terrified of turning into a religious freak.'

'You won't turn into anything you don't want to turn into,' Charles reassured me. Neil came in, and the conversation turned to more general topics.

I found it comforting, though, having Charles call in every so often, and I had his phone number at Teen Challenge. It made me feel secure. He knew where I was at and he could handle me, even when I was throwing tantrums.

A few days later an attractive woman with greying hair appeared at the door. 'Hello,' she greeted me warmly. 'You must be Jodie. I'm Rita

Ringma, Charles' wife. I teach pottery here most Tuesdays. Are you going to join us?'

I liked Rita. She was warm, vibrant and somehow comfortable to be with. I enjoyed starting to learn pottery. It was quite exciting to create something beautiful out of a lump of clay. I began to look forward to Tuesdays.

Most nights I still had terrifying nightmares. One night I dreamed I was walking along a dark, narrow street in Kings Cross. Suddenly Mum was there talking to me and I was so glad to see her I was really bubbling over. I was leading her back to my flat, talking excitedly. Then I turned and looked at her and it wasn't my mother any more, but that kinky guy who'd followed me. I began to run, but his footsteps were following me. He was getting closer, closer . . . I was running as fast as I could, gasping frantically for breath. I awoke streaming perspiration and calling out, 'Mum, Mum!'

'It's okay, Jodie,' replied a soothing, motherly voice. It was Margie. I began to sob and sob. Margie sat on the edge of the bed and stroked my hair, just like a mother, till I stopped shaking and eventually fell asleep again.

There were several of these encounters with Margie in the night. Every time she'd hear me scream in my sleep, she'd get out of bed in the cold and sit with me.

Everything was going quite well and I was getting used to the people there. Then I hit a brick wall unexpectedly.

We were given jobs on a roster basis and kept the same job for a week. One Monday morning one of the workers, Mike, was announcing the jobs. 'It's your turn to clean the toilets, Jodie,' he said calmly.

I stared at him. He couldn't be for real. Didn't he have any idea what I'd been through? 'No way,' I said flatly.

'I'm sorry, Jodie,' he insisted gently, 'but everyone has to have a turn. I know it's not the most pleasant job.'

Suddenly the old anger was there again. Blinding, uncontrollable fury sweeping through me like a bushfire out of control. I began yelling at Mike and hurling abuse of every kind at him. A torrent of the vilest swear words poured out of me. This went on for about five minutes. Maybe longer. I barely registered Margie's whitened face looking at me with pleading eyes.

After calling Mike all the names I could think of, I began to sob while I was still screaming. 'And you're all a bunch of filthy hypocrites,' I sobbed, 'or you wouldn't expect me to do something like that.'

My whole life at Koinonia crumbled around me and I collapsed in a sobbing heap. I felt an arm around me. It was Margie. But I was too shattered to look at her. She was one of 'them'.

'Jodie, come in here,' Sue said in a firm but gentle voice. She led me into the living room and closed the door. 'Jodie, part of the agreement you make when you live here is to participate in the work roster. We've all got our pet hates. You know how Billie hates cooking, but she has to do it, like everyone else.

'I'm not cleaning the toilets,' I choked out.

Sue sighed. 'Okay. So what have you got against it? None of us like it, that's for sure. I suppose it's beneath your dignity?'

'That's not the problem,' I said abruptly.

'Look, we're going to sort this out even if I sit here all day with you,' said Sue. 'So you may as well be honest about it.'

'I am being honest.'

'Well, what's it all about?'

I'm trapped. I'm going to have to tell her. No. Why the hell should I? It's none of her business. I suppose they'll chuck me out of this place if I don't tell her. What am I going to do?

I took a deep breath. Okay, she'd asked for it. So I'd tell her. 'It's not just the job of cleaning. It's the whole thing about toilets. The number of times I locked myself in the toilet to get away from some creepy client. Look, I'd huddle in that toilet and I'd hear him shouting for me to come out. It was terrifying. And when I finally did come out, if he was still there, I'd get beaten up.'

Sue sighed sympathetically.

'And that's not the only thing,' I continued.

'Often I'd go into a toilet to shoot up heroin. Every time I go into the toilets, I think of all those times, huddling and shivering with some half-mental guy outside, or shooting up. And, to cap it all off, often we'd hang around public toilets to pick up clients. So,' by this time I was calmer and was talking in a blunt, almost scathing voice, 'you can see why I don't like toilets. It's like walking into a nightmare every time I go there.'

Sue's eyes were moist. 'I'll discuss it with Neil,' she said. 'I'll see you after lunch.'

After lunch she called me over. 'Jodie, we've discussed it and we really understand, but we feel it's important for you to go through with it. Better to overcome it now, while you've got friends around you, than to avoid it all your life.'

'Friends!' I snapped. 'You've got a funny idea of friends, when you know what this means to me.'

'I'm sorry, but it's for your own good,' Sue replied.

So I cleaned the toilets. It was that or split. My mind was tormented with hideous memories the whole time.

Later that night, Margie asked me about it, so I told her what I'd told Sue.

'Oh, Jodie,' Margie said, 'I wish I could clean them for you. I'd be happy to, you know. You've suffered so much already. But you'll just have to go through with it. God will probably use it to help you get over some of those awful memories.'

I grunted cynically, but I was touched that this amazing lady would be willing to clean the toilets for me. I knew she meant it. Surprisingly, it did get a little easier after a while, but the first few times were gruelling.

The weeks were passing. Strange how clear everything seemed now. I was getting to know the others at Koinonia and really liked most of them. They were real people. I was a real person.

Days and nights no longer seemed a jumble of meaningless events. Everything seemed somehow clear, definite. Time wasn't a confusing muddle, but a more leisurely sequence of days and weeks that were, on the whole, fairly happy.

Apart from Margie, I gravitated most towards Rick. Rick had been on smack, too. He'd been part of the Sydney scene; in and out of jail for drug dealing and burglary. But he was fun. He bore no resemblance to the hard-eyed drug dealers I'd known in the Cross. It was such a relief, too, to have someone else there who'd come from a scene pretty much like mine. We began to spend quite a bit of our free time together. I'd found another real friend. Strange how he'd been part of that scene and yet now he was one of 'them', a religious freak. I grappled to understand this apparent contradiction, but even Margie's explanations didn't totally resolve it for me. So I shelved it. Perhaps I'd understand some time later.

My conversations with Margie continued. I pestered her more and more with questions about religion, despite my fear of becoming a religious freak. But I wanted to understand what made these peaceful, happy people tick.

Two months passed. Each morning we all had to go to a Bible study. In these sessions and in various discussions I began to understand who Jesus was. He was not just some good guy who'd lived a couple of thousand years ago, nor was he a God who lived in peace up in heaven and left us to sweat it out for ourselves on earth. He really cared about us and wanted to help us in our daily lives. He had been crucified so our sins could be forgiven and he wanted us to give our lives to him and to follow his teachings. He even wanted to heal the hurts from our past. There were all sorts of things he wanted us to do, too, like forgiving the people who'd hurt us and ripped us off. That really blew me out. It was a bit much to expect, but every time I found something hard to understand or to accept, I'd talk it through with Margie. I came to understand that Jesus actually gives Christians his Spirit to live inside them, and that's why they were so happy and peaceful and could handle things better than I could. The idea of having hope for the future—the immediate future and forever—was appealing, too. And apparently, God actually had a purpose and plan for each person's life.

So when, one evening during a long discussion, Margie asked me, 'Do you feel ready to give your life to Jesus and make a Christian commitment, Jodie? Do you want to?' I didn't react adversely. I appreciated that nobody had tried to force me to ask God to forgive me or anything.

'You guys have got something I want.' I admitted. 'You're all so happy and you really care about one another. Even about me. I haven't got what you've got.'

'You're no different from us,' Margie assured me. 'God loves you just as much as he loves us.'

I hesitated for a moment. My past life flashed before me. To become a Christian . . . this certainly wasn't what I'd planned or even hoped for. I guess I'd really hoped it wouldn't happen. But it was different now that I understood who Jesus really was. And Christianity certainly wasn't a cult. These people were normal people —happy ones.

Now I understood that God genuinely wanted good things for me. He didn't want me to keep on living in torment. It was pretty mind-boggling. But was there any other way I could go? Could I live a happy life without being a Christian? Part of me still wanted to say 'Yes' to that, but even that part seemed to be stilled into submission that evening.

'Well, I give up,' I said. 'What do I have to do?'

'Just ask Jesus to forgive you,' she said. 'Thank him for dying on the cross for you and carrying the price of your sins, and ask him to come into your life.'

So I knelt down and began to pray.

God, I'm doing it. I'm giving my life to you. I wonder if there'll be thunder and lightning or something. A voice from the sky, maybe? Will I be totally different after this?

There was no thunder or lightning. Just a quiet transaction between me and God. Then a peace flooded my being. It felt so wonderful and it's been with me, except on rare occasions, ever since.

That was the amazing thing. Even though I was still struggling a bit in myself, God did it anyway. He took me just as I was and filled me with his life and peace.

The next day, as I sat in the garden thinking, talking to God, and writing in the diary I'd recently begun, I noticed everything seemed more beautiful than ever. The flowering shrubs along the driveway were glowing in pink profusion. Even the grass seemed greener, softer, more vibrant. I began gathering flowers for the living room.

Silken sunlight slipping through my fingers. Silvery shafts of light gleaming through the trees. I'm a new person. The Bible says so. A whole new creation with a whole new life ahead of me. A life without dope; with Jesus to help me instead. I'm free. No more prison bars. Nothing can spoil this peace and my beautiful new life now.

Several happy weeks later, Neil called me into his office. 'Jodie, your court case is coming up in Sydney in a few weeks. I've just received notice that you have to be there.'

'What court case?' I stared at him in horror. 'I thought all that had been fixed up.'

'The charges for drug using have been paid off, but apparently there was a charge for breaking and entering, as well. Maybe you didn't realise at the time.'

I felt as if I'd been kicked in the stomach.

'I've spoken to Margie,' Neil continued. 'She'll go down to Sydney with you, so you'll be all right. You can stay with our friends in the Bible College for a few nights. We'll all be praying for you.'

I walked out feeling almost stunned. How did this fit into my new Christian life?

That night I lay awake long into the night thinking about Sydney and the court case. Would God fight for me so I didn't have to go to gaol? How would I feel about seeing my old 'friends' and the whole Sydney scene? And another more insidious thought was creeping into my consciousness—heroin.

Chapter Twelve

The bus roared and plunged through the night, tunnelling relentlessly through the darkness towards Sydney. At my side, Margie dozed intermittently, but I couldn't sleep. My stomach was tied in a knot of fear. Terrifying thoughts crowded my mind in confusion.

What was to stop me, once I was in Sydney, from going straight back into my old scene? I'd changed a lot, for sure, but was this who I really was? I would have to find out. When we arrived, I would look up my old friends just to see how I really felt about it all. To see whether I still wanted dope or not and whether I was throwing my life away, living with a bunch of Christians in Brisbane.

Margie seemed a bit tense. Perhaps she sensed some of what I was thinking.

In the first hours of daylight we hit the northern suburbs of Sydney and soon pulled into the terminus. We staggered out, straightening our stiffened limbs after the long journey, then climbed into a car waiting to take us to stay at a Bible College near Sydney.

The guy driving us was a friendly, sincere Christian. I felt uncomfortable with him and wondered if he could tell what I was thinking.

Soon we were settled into a simple, comfortable room with a magnificent view of mountains and valleys. 'Let's go for a walk after lunch,' Margie suggested. 'This is a really beautiful place.'

I readily agreed. Anything to tear my mind from clutching obsessively at my old scene, and smack. It was a bright, sunny day in August and the mountains were an intense blue against the clear sky. We talked as we walked, but all the time I was talking, the familiar old thoughts tugged at my mind.

Heroin. It was like heaven. But I don't need it any more now. My life isn't hell any longer. Not most of the time, anyway. I just want to check the scene out; see whether I've really made the right decision. I'm strong enough now not to give in to it if I don't want to. But I'm scared. Scared of how I'll really react. I feel as if something's pulling me back to the

Cross ... and to smack.

Margie was keen to have an early night after our bus trip, so we settled down soon after tea. A few hours later, I tiptoed across the room. She was fast asleep. Really out to it. I grabbed some clothes and quickly, quietly dressed. Moving almost silently, I slipped out the door, closed it and ran out into the night.

I jumped on a train, then a bus, and was soon in the Cross. Excitement was beginning to well up inside me. I headed straight for Chris' and Liz's flat. Surely they'd be glad to see me now, after all this time. I was so much more together now, too. That should impress them.

There were several of the old crowd there at the flat and they had smack. Jim waved some under my nose. 'Missing it, eh, Jodie?' he taunted.

It was too much for me. I'd have a taste. Just one. It was still bliss. Nothing mattered any more. So before long I had some more. My money soon ran out and there were no more free tastes offering, so the following night I went back onto the streets and picked up some clients.

I feel as if I'm an animal being hunted; as if the shadows are going to leap up and grab me. But this is who I really am. I've got some really nice friends and a cosy little life at

Koinonia, but that's not the real me. This is the lifestyle I'm used to.

I stayed with Chris and Liz and worked on the streets for three nights. The mental torment that gripped me was intolerable. I kept getting a mental image of God crying—crying over me.

Guilt and confusion would almost crush me. There were other voices talking to me inside my head. 'Come on, Jodie,' the voices would say, 'this is who you are. Forget about Brisbane. This scene is the real thing.' So I'd shoot up more heroin to avoid facing the torment and conflict.

God, I feel guilty; feel as if I've ripped you off —just used you and dumped you. But that's stupid. I don't suppose you'd really care anyway. I'm just not the kind of person that you'd want to know. I've tried, but I can't be.

After three nights of working on the streets, it was time for my court case. I was dreading it, hoping I wouldn't get chucked into prison. I thought Margie would have given up on me by now and gone back to Brisbane, so I felt small, alone and defiant as I faced the judge.

Suddenly I looked across the room. Margie was there. A pale-faced, sad-eyed Margie. I caught her eye and tears began to run down her cheeks. I clenched my fists, but in spite of my efforts, and the smack I'd had, I started crying too.

The sight of my tears did nothing to soften the judge. He just annihilated me. Verbally whipped me and tore me to shreds. I felt humiliated and broken inside. And the sight of Margie there had done something to me. I felt convicted by God. I had let him down . . . and Margie . . . and myself . . . and all the people at Teen Challenge who'd helped me so much. What I was doing was sin; dirty, filthy sin.

When the judge had finished his verbal lashing, he let me off with a fine.

Margie was waiting for me outside on the corner. I could hardly look at her without crying, but I steeled myself to meet her earnest gaze. Her big brown eyes implored me sadly out of her pale, drained face.

'Which way are you going to go, Jodie?' she asked in a quiet voice. 'Are you coming the narrow road or are you going to take the wide road?'

I had to make a decision then and there on the footpath. It was the hardest decision I'd ever made in my life, standing there on that corner with people pushing past me.

My throat constricted as I tried to talk. At last I choked out, 'I'm going the wide road.' She grew paler. I continued, 'I can't go back. I'm too dirty now. It's too late. I've had a taste of it and I've got to go back into it.' My eyes were filling with tears again.

'Well, I'm still at the college. I'll be getting the bus back to Brisbane tonight,' said Margie in a lifeless voice.

Tears streamed down my face and I turned quickly away from her and walked back through the city crying.

Chapter Thirteen

People pushed past me and bumped into me as I walked shakily through town. Several people looked quizzically at my tear-streaked face. I ignored them. I had to get back to the girls' flat.

I've blown it. God wouldn't want me back now. I've gone too far. And this whole scene is too familiar. It's where I belong. It's the real me. I know this world better than that other world in Brisbane. I can't live up to what God wants me to be. It was really pleasant at Koinonia, but that's not who I really am.

Back at Chris' and Liz's flat I sat down, exhausted and drained after the court case, and prepared to relax over a cup of coffee. But something was wrong. Here I was, back in my old scene, on home ground with the court case out of the way, and smack available whenever I wanted it. I wasn't hanging out for a fix, but I could get no peace at all—only intolerable conflict and misery. I couldn't live with myself. Something indefinable was tugging at my heart and mind; tugging so hard I couldn't bear it. I knew it was tied up with God and Margie and Koinonia. So I had one last hit of heroin and took a taxi to the College to see Margie. She wouldn't be leaving for a few hours yet.

Tentatively, I opened the door, then hurried to Margie's room. She was visibly shaken at my sudden appearance and seemed to be fighting tears.

'Look,' I said, 'I don't know why I've come to see you. I just don't know what to do. Should I come back with you, or not? Is it too late? Is there any hope for me? Am I throwing my life away, coming to Brisbane? I can't make the decision. You make it for me. Please. If I stay here, I know I haven't got much, but at least it's all familiar to me. If I go back with you, I don't really feel as if I'll ever be good enough. How am I ever going to live down what I've done? Is it worth my going back there?'

Margie grabbed my arm. 'Yes, yes,' she said pleadingly. 'You're coming back with me. Please don't throw your life away. Jodie, you *can* make it. Please, please don't give up.'

I couldn't believe this woman could care so much for me after what I'd done. All my arguments and questions dissolved before the intensity of her plea.

I went back to Brisbane with Margie. It was another gruelling bus trip. I felt so condemned about what I'd done in Sydney. How could I ever face Neil and Sue? And Rick? And all the others? What would Charles say? They'd all trusted me to come down here and I'd blown it ... totally.

We arrived at the bus depot late in the afternoon. Neil and Sue were there to pick us up. Neil smiled at me and he and Sue hugged us both. Sue's eyes were a bit troubled or was it just my imagination? Did they know? Had Margie rung them and told them? Why hadn't I thought of that and asked her? Perhaps everyone already knew. Maybe they would ask me to leave. I'd let them down badly.

I was silent as we drove to Koinonia. One look at my miserable face probably told everyone without my saying a word. I became increasingly anxious. I didn't know what they would think, or what they were thinking. So, after tea that night, I told everyone what had happened in Sydney. 'So', I concluded miserably, 'I've really blown it and let you guys down.'

When I'd finished talking, I waited, cringing inwardly, for the rebuking words that would fall like blows on my already crushed emotions. Or, worse still, for a long silence and averted eyes.

Instead, Neil spoke first. 'You haven't let us down, Jodie. It's only yourself you've let down. But don't be too hard on yourself. It was a very difficult test for a new Christian. You blew it initially, sure. We all fail some of our tests. But you came through the real test by deciding to come back. You haven't "blown it" now. We love you and we want you here.'

Sue quickly echoed Neil's words of forgiveness and all the others joined in with words of forgiveness, encouragement, reassurance. I could hardly believe it. Every single one of them forgave me and accepted me back as one of them, just as if it had never happened. That just blew me out. I knew then I could never leave my Christian family at Koinonia. Not till it was the time for me to go on to something else ... something Christian.

At least I'll never have to wonder again how I'd feel about the Sydney scene. I've had a taste of it. It's exactly the same as it always was: the terror at night in the streets; the great escape into heroin; and the aching void inside me.

I settled back into the routine at Koinonia and soon I was back to the happy, fairly peaceful life I'd had before the court case.

But several things still bothered me. Nightmares continued to torment me most nights and memories of Jonothan and Roxy still nagged at my mind. It concerned me, also, that I couldn't make any sense out of the Bible. All the others believed it implictly, read it daily, and often used it as a sort of textbook on how to live their lives. But I couldn't understand it; couldn't believe the God of the Bible would love me. How could he, if he were perfect and holy and all that?

I was a bit unnerved, too, at how easily I'd gone back into drugs and prostitution. It had been as if a sinister, irresistible force were pulling me. Could it happen to me again? I knew the scene held nothing for me, but what if that force started drawing me back? Would I be able to resist it?

Chapter Fourteen

'Jodie,' said Charles a few days later, on one of his visits to Koinonia, 'how would you like to be prayer-counselled?'

I looked at him blankly.

'Prayer-counselled?' I echoed.

'Yes. It's a special form of prayer and counselling. The counsellors are all trained, but they let the Holy Spirit lead them as they pray for you.'

I hesitated. It sounded a bit spooky.

'I think you'd benefit from it enormously,' Charles continued.

A date was set, and a few weeks later I found myself sitting in a cosy little room under the Ringmas' house, with Charles and another lady sitting on chairs on either side of me. Charles introduced me to Jill, the lady beside me. Upstairs, Rita Ringma and a few others were praying. They'd all put aside the whole day, just to pray for me.

First they led me to renounce all my occult and sexual involvements. As I renounced each thing and asked God's forgiveness, they prayed for me. Then Charles said, 'I have the impression that God is saying he wanted you to be a girl. It was his special choice for you.'

Tears filled my eyes as I remembered the many years of trying to be one of the boys, striving to gain Mum's affection and all the time, God had wanted me to be a girl. I began to cry, and cried till I couldn't cry any more.

Then came a blow. 'God wants you to forgive your mother, Jodie,' said Charles, 'for everything she did and everything she didn't do.'

I sat and stared at Charles and Jill. My fists were clenched with the familiar anger. 'Why the hell should I?' I asked. 'She doesn't deserve to be forgiven. She couldn't care whether I forgave her or not.'

'No, but God does care,' said Jill firmly, 'and it's affecting your whole outlook on life, too. God requires us to forgive everyone who's wronged us, before we can receive full forgiveness.'

'Why?'

'Well, he's forgiven you a lot, hasn't he? He's given you a chance to start all over again with a

When the prayer-counselling was over, I was exhausted. But I felt strangely warm and peaceful inside like I'd never felt before.

That night I picked up my Bible and it was like a different book. It made more sense. I couldn't wait to read more of it, and I was overcome with awe and gratitude as I realised that God really did love me. His love was a different kind of love from anything I'd ever known. A love that could forgive me for selling the body he'd created and for everything else I'd done. I'd never been able to believe this before. And he'd wanted me to be a girl. It wasn't just an accident. I was a proper woman, planned by God.

The very next day I flew to New Zealand to visit my mother who was remarrying. She was astonished at my appearance. 'Jodie...' she seemed at a loss for words. 'You're not so skinny any more. You've even got colour in your cheeks. And,' she paused, then said tentatively, 'you look happy. What's happened?'

So I told her about my conversion to Christianity. I noticed she was fighting tears at times.

'You know my sister, your aunt in Queensland?' she asked.

'You mean John's mother? The one we stayed with when I was a teenager?'

'Yes. Well, she's been praying for you ever since we visited them, she says. Isn't that funny. She asks after you every time she writes to me, and always says she's praying for you. All these years she's been saying that.'

A lump came into my throat and I swallowed, remembering that kind, friendly aunt I'd visited and the incredible feeling of warmth and peace I'd felt there.

It was amazing to be talking to my mother without feeling angry or bitter. I felt a genuine caring for her and hoped she, too, would become a Christian before long. I wondered if my praying aunt was praying for Mum as well as for me. No doubt she knew, from John, about my initial attempted conversion and my shaky beginnings with him. I would ring my cousin John and tell him how I was now as soon as I returned to Brisbane.

I told Roger my story, too. He was sceptical, but the change in me set him thinking.

Returning to Koinonia was like going home. I felt quite elated as I greeted each one of my 'family' there and was welcomed back. I looked around the table at teatime. There was Neil, quiet and intelligent, gently but firmly leading us all. And Susie, his wife. Susie, who had initially aroused my suspicion and animosity, and later my jealousy over her apparently secure life with a nice husband and three lovely children. I realised I'd grown fond of Susie. We'd clashed many times as I'd bucked against various things (like the toilet-cleaning crisis), but she'd never given up on me. She just kept on forgiving me as I blundered along.

Then there was Rick, of course. I was really quite attached to him as we had such similar backgrounds and he was a strong, likeable guy. Beside Rick sat Mike, a worker there like Margie. A nice guy. A bit wary of me as if he thought I was going to erupt. Then there was Don, sitting there half-heartedly nibbling his dinner. Poor guy, he'd been in and out of psychiatric hospitals and had played with various kinds of drugs. He was fun, though. I enjoyed his quaint sense of humour and felt for him in his struggles. There was Wayne, a slightly older man, battling alcoholism. He was a good bloke, too. Had a heart of gold. Judy, a single mother, smiled at me warmly from beside Wayne. I hadn't really had a chance to get to know her very well, but she was part of my new family and seemed nice. The only person I still found hard to handle was Cameron, a tall, lanky guy who had been into everything from grass to cough mixture. Not smack though. He thought he was a real intellectual and was always in his head. Sometimes he'd punctuate a perfectly normal conversation with some way-out, cryptic comment that was meant to be clever, but it always annoyed me. I realised, though, that even he didn't make me feel really angry now. In fact, I felt almost a warmth towards him; towards all my Koinonia family.

Faithful Margie sat beside me, merrily chattering as we ate. She seemed delighted to have me back there. It was wonderful to see her. I felt a complete sense of belonging.

A few days later I rang John from Koinonia,

wondering how he would feel about me after our rocky relationship several months back. There was no trace of reserve in his voice. He was delighted to hear how I was and where I was. He even came out to visit me and I found him friendly and easy to relate to this time.

After a few weeks back at Koinonia, Margie said, 'Jodie, do you realise you haven't had one nightmare since the prayer-counselling? Well, not that I know of, anyway.'

I thought for a minute, 'No, I haven't. Isn't that incredible!' I realised that I no longer dreaded the dark and the hideous memories and distortions that had tormented my mind night after night. I actually had been sleeping peacefully for two whole weeks and I continued to do so.

I enjoyed the days there. In particular, I loved the creative things that had been introduced into my life: pottery, writing, drawing, arranging flowers.

God, is this what happiness is? It must be. I enjoy being alive; and I never wanted to live before. All those years, trapped in that mind-bending torment of not wanting to live but being terrified to die. I'm glad to be alive now. I'm even glad to be a girl. Funny, I hardly ever think about Jono or Roxy any more. It's not that I don't love them any more. But before it was as if they were with me all the time. I could never get away from their faces. Didn't even want to. But they're gone now. I'm sad about them; really sad. But I'm me, and I've got a life to live. That's the first time I've ever felt like that. I'm a real person with a life of my own—a life that I actually want.

Not that life was without struggles. I guess I wouldn't have been me if I'd just floated through everything. From time to time I still dug my heels in over various household issues and clashed with some of the others there. My colourful vocabulary did not entirely desert me. I was not one to give in to change easily, even when God himself instigated the changes. But on the whole it was a very happy time. The daily Bible studies and discussion groups helped me to apply Christianity and Jesus to my daily life. It certainly wasn't anything airy-fairy I'd been brought into.

Soon after my trip to New Zealand, I began to sense I needed more of God's life and power in me to enable me to follow Jesus better and to be able to serve him. I had a growing desire to really serve him in some way. So some of the people at Koinonia prayed for me and I was baptised in the Holy Spirit. This added a whole new dimension to my ability to pray and to love people, and I found I could face life's challenges more easily. I became calmer and happier, but my basic volatile nature never disappeared. One thing was for sure, life would never be dull for me or for those around me!

Daily life continued to present me with new challenges, questions and discoveries. Margie and I were having one of our many talks one day, when she smiled and said, 'There's another important step now.'

'What's that?' I asked.

'I think it's time you were baptised in water.'

She explained its significance to me. It sounded exciting. To do something that symbolised the death and burial of my old life and my rebirth to life as a new person.

'Where would they baptise me?' I asked.

'Well, we've got a camp coming up soon, in Numinbah Valley. Lots of people from Jubilee Fellowship and Teen Challenge are coming. There's a beautiful creek with a big swimming hole there. I think Charles is planning to have a baptismal service.'

I was excited as I packed for the camp. I had a feeling that this would be a real turning point; an announcement for all those people to see, that the old Jodie—the junkie, the street worker—was gone, buried with Christ, and that a whole new Jodie was alive, living in the resurrection power of Jesus.

The camp site at Nerang Wood was beautiful. Tree-clad mountains towered around a peaceful, brilliantly green valley, with the glistening river winding lazily through it. Everything was so quiet and still. I heard birds singing and twittering in the morning when I awoke and sun streamed in through the small window.

That afternoon about seventy people gathered beside the pool. Several of us were to be baptised. We sang for a while and again I found myself crying. Crying, but not feeling sad. Just overwhelmed with love and gratitude to God and these amazing people.

Charles read some Scriptures about baptism and then it was time for us to go into the water. I waded happily out to where Charles and Neil stood waist deep in water. Charles prayed briefly as he and Neil gently pushed me under the water and pulled me up.

God, I really mean this. I want to be a new person. I want to keep on loving you, and to do something for you; something to thank you. I want to serve you in some way. Sunlight glistening through water as I burst through the surface up into the light again. Sunlight on my face like God smiling on me as I do this. Everyone's singing about Jesus. I feel so light and happy.

Half-laughing with sheer delight, I splashed my way back to the shore. Margie hugged me, even though I was dripping wet. Then Suzie. Then Rita. Nobody seemed to care if they got wet.

I sailed through the rest of the camp so elated I could barely contain my feelings.

From the time I was baptised, I felt really free. For the first time, I knew with a certainty that I was 'the real me' now, living as a Christian. A girl. A daughter of the living God. Kings Cross and the streets and smack were no longer part of my identity.

'But you'll have to come to terms with the fact that it will often involve decisions of your own will,' Charles explained. 'You may face times of difficulty in life when an escape into heroin would seem quite appealing. But it would be a costly escape. Too costly. Jesus will always be there to help you to resist it, if you're willing.'

I realised he was right, though at the moment I had no desire for smack or my old life. So I resolved to see it through, going straight, and to ask God to help me if ever I were tempted. And as I thought about it, I knew that the sinister force that had pulled me back so recently was gone. I could view the situation almost objectively. Relief flooded my mind.

One day I decided to make a card for Margie, to thank her for everything she'd done for me. I carefully glued dried flowers onto the front and wrote a poem inside it. It was one of the first things I had ever done for anybody out of genuine love and gratitude. What would she think? Would she think it was silly?

I left it on her bed that evening and disappeared to the bathroom. When I returned, she was sitting on the bed with tears in her eyes. 'It's beautiful,' she said, and hugged me. 'I'll always keep it.'

I felt so warm inside, I wanted to laugh or cry

or something. So I made a few more cards for some of the others there. I was amazed at how much I enjoyed doing it.

Little by little, I came to realise that I actually loved my 'family' at Koinonia and, much to my surprise, they all seemed to love me. I'd become friendly with a few other girls at Jubilee Fellowship, too. People genuinely seemed to like me. Sometimes it overwhelmed me.

Many afternoons, when I wasn't doing chores or pottery, I'd sit in the garden writing or drawing. It was so peaceful.

Sometimes, still, I'd collect flowers, ferns and prettily-shaped twigs and decorate the living room, or just sit for a while on the grassy banks, watching the big brown river flow quietly by.

I can enjoy just sitting and looking at nature, now. I'm at peace with myself and with God. All the anger's gone out of me. All my life I've been desperate and searching for an answer for that desperation ... and anything to fill the great gaping emptiness inside me. Nothing ever did. Not drugs, sex ... nothing. I was always running away; running away from the pain of being alive. Knowing something was missing and not knowing what it was. I'm not empty inside any more. I feel completely satisfied. There's nothing to run away from now. I love being alive.

A few people had come and gone already in

the six months I'd been there. I was determined to stick it out for the recommended twelve months, though. If I could stay straight that long, I'd have a better chance of staying out of smack and the whole scene when I left Koinonia. Most of the time it wasn't like a rehab centre at all. They really had succeeded in making it a home. I was happy to stay.

> *God, I really love these people. Isn't that amazing. It's me, Jodie, the real me, and I really love them. I'm glad I've got you to talk to as well, through Jesus. It helps. Just knowing that you understand me, even when I blow it. One thing I've noticed, you've really helped me to accept my lot as a single person and stop resenting Susie for everything she's got in life. Maybe you'll have a husband for me one day. That'd be wonderful. Imagine ... me, actually thinking marriage would be good. It's taken me so long to get used to guys even touching me on the arm without reacting. I don't suppose I'll be able to have children, after wrecking my insides by working the streets for so long. Still ... God, you could heal me I suppose. It'd be so nice to have a husband and children. Not yet, though. I need a bit longer to get myself together and to get it together with you, Lord.*

I walked slowly up the grassy banks, back to the house. I'd been through so much in my first six months here. Hopefully the next six months would be a bit more peaceful. Not boring, but no more major dramas . . . hopefully.

Chapter Fifteen

The long summer days were peaceful and, for the most part, very happy. Neil and Sue were leaving at the end of the year and a new couple were replacing them. This caused some upheaval amongst us.

Rick, particularly, seemed disturbed. He had become rather moody lately and I was concerned about him. One afternoon, when he was gardening, he called me over from where I was cleaning a window. 'I'm going to split,' he told me fiercely. 'Do you want to come?'

'Come where?' I asked nervously.

'Back to Sydney. I've had this place. I'm not going to be shoved around by new people I don't even know. This place is starting to get to me, anyway.'

I was shaken and angry. 'Don't be so stupid, Rick,' I whispered hoarsely. 'You'd never handle the temptation. Not yet, anyway.'

'I'm not dumb enough to get sucked back into the old scene,' Rick said unconvincingly.

I went back to cleaning my window and began to ask God what to do. Should I tell Neil and risk losing Rick's trust and friendship? Perhaps I should for Rick's sake. I walked inside and found Neil. By the time I had told him and we had gone out to the garden, Rick had disappeared.

Neil went to his room. 'He's gone,' he said sadly. 'He must have had his gear packed already.'

That was the last I heard of Rick for many months and when I finally heard, the news wasn't good. He was back into dope.

A few of the others left, too, with the impending change of leadership. But at least they talked it through with Neil, who found suitable places for them to live with Christians. And they'd been at Koinonia longer and were just about ready to leave anyway. I decided to stick out my twelve months, as I'd planned, and do my best to adapt to new leaders.

As it turned out, the new leaders were really nice, and I enjoyed my last four months there.

Then, suddenly, from being a quiet, secluded, little pool of security in lovely old Graceville, we were plummeted into the news. Heroin and drugs in general were headlines of the daily papers. Bob Hawke's daughter was a drug addict. (She came off drugs and was rehabilitated.) Bob Hawke was distressed. Much of Australia was shocked and distressed. Suddenly Australia was face to face with problems it could no longer hide, or push away into the dingy back streets of its cities—problems for which it was looking for answers. Several TV channels rang Neil, who now worked in the Teen Challenge office, and they came and interviewed him.

Neil rang me. 'Jodie,' he asked tentatively, 'how would you feel about doing a television interview for one of the current affairs programmes? And a couple of newspapers would like articles, too.'

I was silent, thinking.

'I'll ring you back tonight. Think about it. I know it mightn't be easy, but you might help someone.'

My mind was in turmoil. How could I appear on television and let everyone look at me like some sort of circus freak? How could I believe in myself as a new person while people were pointing at me and saying, 'She's the one who was a prostitute, a heroin addict?' What if someone like Tom in Sydney saw the programme and came up here to hassle me and try to get me back on the streets? Dozens of questions whirled around my mind.

Then another thought came into focus: the girls on the streets. They needed to hear what I had to say. Here in Brisbane, in the Cross, anywhere. Who was going to tell them how to find a better way of life? I thought of Roxy, dead. And Shana and Kelly. It was too late for them, now. But there were still Chris and Liz and dozens of others I knew, and hundreds more I didn't know. Someone had to tell them, and they weren't likely to take much notice of some totally straight chick who'd never been to hell and back, like I had.

The doubts and questions grew less persistent as I formed a clear decision. I wanted to tell them. I actually wanted to witness to them. I wanted God to use me and to use everything I'd lived through to help others. For some time I had felt I wanted to serve God in some way, to thank him for all he'd done for me. Now I knew this must be part of it; an important part. Yes I would tell them. Tell them about me and about Jesus and what he had done for me; what he could do for them.

So when Neil rang back, somewhat to his surprise, I said, 'Yes.'

I dressed nervously for the television interview. This would be hard. Margie was coming with me. I don't think I could have coped without her.

It wasn't as bad as I expected. Neil had asked them not to let the public see my face, for my own protection, so they interviewed me with my back to the cameras.

There was only one other media interview.

Teen Challenge policy protected new Christians from becoming 'superstars'. They figured, probably rightly, we were better off without too much publicity. Charles and Neil both said they were keen for me, and for all of us, to make normal lives for ourselves, and being in the limelight too much wouldn't help.

It was a strange feeling, though. Suddenly, after being part of the 'dregs of society', I was being applauded, encouraged, even admired. I had succeeded in something important.

The new leaders were keen to have a graduation dinner for me when my twelve months were completed in April. I was thrilled. I loved special occasions at Koinonia. I enjoyed decorating the house with flowers, both fresh and dried, and preparing nice food ... making everything look beautiful. Susie's sister had been married at Koinonia, and I'd loved making the place really special and festive for the occasion.

Now it was my 'occasion', but still I wanted to help with the decor. Creating, whether it was decorating, writing, pottery or whatever, still gave me tremendous satisfaction. So a few of us made the place as beautiful as possible; specially the big living room with its doors opening out onto the patio overlooking the river.

I had hand-made invitations for a few of my special friends who had left, including Neil and Sue. They were all coming. Margie and I had bought a new dress for me. It was the most feminine dress I'd ever owned; soft cream Indian cotton with embroidery.

The night arrived. I looked at my reflection in the mirror. My cheeks were flushed with excitement. I looked so different from the Jodie of a year ago. I'd gained weight. Not too much, but I was no longer skinny. The dress made me look and feel almost like a bride.

The guests were arriving. There was Charles, his brown eyes sometimes thoughtful, sometimes twinkling. Rita, looking as attractive as ever, hugging me effusively. I could almost feel the warmth and love flowing through her into me. Then Jill and her husband, Albert. More hugs. More love. And Neil and Sue looking so proud of me, as if I were one of their own daughters.

After we'd had a festive meal together, I stood up and briefly gave my testimony. Then one after another people stood up and said things about me. I was overwhelmed. Nobody tried to pretend I was perfect but they said so many special things. Neil and Sue applauded my stickability and courage for seeing it through and staying straight. Rita said how much she'd enjoyed teaching me pottery and how many creative gifts I had. It seemed that everyone had something good to say. Then Margie stood up. What could she say? Surely it had all been said.

'I want to thank Jodie,' she said, 'for being such a special lady and a wonderful friend.' I blinked. *She* was thanking *me* for being a good friend? 'And,' she continued, 'you've taught me so much, Jodie. I've learned through your struggles. I think I've grown and softened through knowing you. Thanks.' She smiled at me with moist eyes.

I was blown out. I wanted to say more, too, so I stood up. 'Look, I really want to thank you guys all over again,' I said. 'When I first came to Teen Challenge, I was desperate, really desperate. I didn't even know who I was any more. But I know who I am now. And Jesus really does set you free, you know. I can be who I really am. I don't have to put up a wall and be so hard that nobody can reach me. Even if someone does hurt me, God can heal me. And God's hand-picked my friends. He's led me into relationships with people I can trust. Some of them have been through a few of the things I've lived through, so they understand me. They know where I'm coming from and I don't feel threatened by the relationships. God's still healing me so I can relate to all different kinds of people. But I'm getting there.

'It's just so good being able to live peacefully myself and with other people. I'm at peace with God. The anger's gone out of me. I didn't want to live, most of my life. I was running away, searching. I'm glad to be alive now. I just want to thank Jesus for giving me life.'

Epilogue

Despite some initial struggles, Jodie continued to live a Christian life and to stay off heroin. When she left Koinonia, she stayed for a while with her 'praying aunt' near Maryborough. Later, after staying a few weeks with Charles and Rita and their four children, she headed out to western Queensland where she worked as a cook on a cattle station. There she joined a Christian group and was encouraged to find herself one of the stronger Christians there. She had been through testings and held on to her faith.

God granted the desires of her heart. It was out in western Queensland that she met the man she later married. She was healed physically, so was able to have children. Now, seven years after her graduation from Koinonia, she and her husband and their two children live in New Zealand and attend a local church there. Jodie is still in touch with Margie (now married also), Charles and Rita, and several of the others who helped her.

Printed in the United States
74129LV00001B/43-51